Your Success Routine: Breakthrough Success with Daily Habits
ISBN: 978-0-9992671-0-3

Copyright © 2025 Charlene Swinton-Witkovic

All rights reserved. No part of this publication may be reproduced, distributed, or transmitted in any form or by any means, including photocopying, recording, or other electronic or mechanical methods, without the prior written permission of the publisher, except in the case of brief quotations embodied in critical reviews and certain other noncommercial uses permitted by copyright law.

Printed in the United States of America

First Edition

Edited by Richard Moore
Published by Self-published

For more information, visit: http://www.breakallbarriers.com

Your Success Routine: Breakthrough Success with Daily Habits

Author: Charlene Swinton-Witkovic
Contributor: **Theresa Mattox**
Contributor: **Ed Witkovic**

Table of Contents

Prologue 5
Message to My Readers 7
Chapter 1: FEAR OF FAILURE 9
Chapter 2: WHEN SELF-DOUBT WHISPERS 14
Chapter 3: SHATTER THE CEILING: REWRITING YOUR BELIEFS 22
Chapter 4: THE POWER OF A CHANGED MIND 28
Chapter 5: CUTTING TIES 56
Chapter 6: BEFORE YOU CAN MOVE FORWARD, YOU MUST KNOW WHAT'S HOLDING YOU BACK 71
Chapter 7: STRATEGIES AND SUPPORT FOR UNSTOPPABLE GROWTH 85
Chapter 8: FOUNDATION OF SUCCESS 97
Chapter 9: DEVELOP THE HABITS OF SUCCESSFUL PEOPLE 105
Chapter 10: BREAKING BARRIERS IN SPECIFIC AREAS 120
Chapter 11: CELEBRATING MILESTONES AND PROGRESS 134
Chapter 12: BUILDING BREAKTHROUGH DAILY HABITS - CHECKLIST FOR READERS: 142
Appendix A 146
Acknowledgments 160
About the Author 161
References 162

Prologue

I remember sitting on a chipped windowsill, the paint peeling beneath my fingers, the faint smell of marijuana drifting in from the hallway. Somewhere down the corridor, someone was laughing. Someone else was yelling. But I didn't move. I just stared out the window as tears traced silent paths down my cheeks.

The world outside seemed unchanged. Cars passed, people rushed by, and clouds drifted across a gray sky. But inside, everything had stopped.

I had just found out I was pregnant. *No money! No plan! No direction! On the edge of homelessness!*

My mother, my anchor, my rock, my everything, had just been diagnosed with cancer. The word hung over us like smoke that wouldn't clear. Even in death, cancer couldn't take her spirit.

School? That wasn't even a thought anymore. It felt like a distant, unreachable planet. I wasn't thinking about essays or lectures. I was thinking about how to eat tomorrow and how to breathe through the next minute. *No money for rent, and nowhere to go. How to survive?*

I looked down at the three pairs of pants I owned: one on me, and two were shared with my sister. We rotated clothes as if it were a game we never agreed to play. My mother was poor in every way—tight, stretched thin, always borrowing.

It wasn't just the pregnancy. It was the weight of everything pressing down at once. The kind of pressure that makes you forget who you were just a week ago. The kind of silence that drowns out even your thoughts. And yet, there I was, just me, my reflection in the glass, and a future I couldn't yet imagine.

Message to My Readers

Congratulations! Whether you know it or not, you have successfully broken down your first of many barriers! Taking the initiative to obtain this book and start this read is not only a clear accomplishment of overcoming inaction, but it should also demonstrate to yourself that you have what it takes to overcome many more barriers in life. Many people love to dream but never take action. They hope that one day all their problems will be solved on their own. It's like a person who spends money every day on the lottery, hoping for that one big win to solve all their problems, rather than taking active steps to develop a budget and improve their financial circumstances. Therefore, "I'm proud to commend you for taking the step to pursue self-improvement."

Your Success Routine: Breakthrough Success with Daily Habits requires action. In researching and studying those who have become phenomenally successful, I realized that, without exception, they had to earn every accomplishment themselves. They overcame numerous barriers to reach where they are today. Their desire for change, paired with a fiery passion for their purpose, propelled them forward despite every obstacle. For many, resilience was forged only after hitting rock bottom and climbing out step by step. Some followed a clear plan, while others adapted as they went, focusing on what they could control. Their steady progress came from an unshakable inner drive and their faith.

The experiences we share from those who have achieved success will not only be inspirational but also provide practical guidance. Each successful person has their own unique set of circumstances—where they started, the challenges they faced along their journey, and how they ultimately achieved success. For some, success shows up externally through career milestones, financial gains, or public recognition. For others, it is deeply internal, reflected in personal growth, peace of mind, or resilience built along the way. And for many, success becomes a legacy—measured by the impact they leave on others and the contributions that outlast them. This diverse collection of experiences provides you with valuable perspectives on how each of them broke down their barriers and defined success on their own terms.

Now it's up to you to decide whether to break the next barrier and complete this book.

Chapter 1: FEAR OF FAILURE

The fear of failure to succeed is deeply rooted in human psychology, and there are several reasons why people experience it. These fears can stem from a combination of personal experiences, societal pressures, and emotional responses. Here are some of the primary reasons why people hesitate to take risks.

People are concerned that they will fail, worry about making mistakes, or face rejection, and this can paralyze them from even starting or trying something new. This feeling often arises from wanting to avoid discomfort or shame.

I can still picture that crisp autumn morning, the classroom was quiet, except for the sound of pages flipping and chairs squeaking. I sat at my desk in second grade, heart pounding, fingers clutching the corner of my first-grade reader. I knew what was coming.

"Charlene," Ms. Wall said, her voice cheery and unaware of the storm inside me, "Would you read the next paragraph, please?"

I stood up slowly. The words on the page looked simple enough. I opened my mouth, trying to sound confident.

"The... straw... stroe... stoebery?"

The moment hung in the air like a bad note.

And then, Ms. Wall burst out laughing. Not a little chuckle—a full, uncontrollable laugh that rocked her body until she leaned on her desk for support.

The class followed.

I stood frozen, cheeks burning, eyes blinking fast to hold back tears. Ms. Wall wiped her eyes and giggled, "Charlene, I think you've invented a new word!". From that day on, *"Stoebery"* became a classroom legend. And I? I became scared of trying. Of speaking. Of failing in front of others.

That one moment followed me like a shadow into adulthood. I didn't always call it fear. Sometimes it looked like overthinking. Sometimes excuses. Sometimes, it's just plain procrastination.

But at the root, it was always the same thing: *What if I try and mess up again?*

I carried that concern with me through college. Central Connecticut State University. A communication major. Two kids. A full-time job. No family support nearby. Just me and the dream of building a better life.

The program was tough. I had to maintain a 3.0 GPA and score high in classes like COMM 140 and COMM 240. For a while, I did.

Until I didn't.

Late nights. Sick kids. Stress. Exhaustion. My grades dropped. And with them came the voice again: *You're not good enough. You're failing. Just quit.*

But I didn't quit. I reached out to professors, tutors, and even the prayer room at the student center. I asked for help and rebuilt my GPA one class at a time.

I started to understand something that took me years to fully believe:

Failure isn't the opposite of success. It's part of it.

Years later, I tried modeling.

I walked into my first agency, nervous but excited. "Turn around," the agent said casually, scanning my figure. Then he dropped a bomb.

"Some clients might want to... touch. Just don't overreact. You'll get blacklisted."

I froze. That wasn't a modeling opportunity. That was a warning disguised as advice. I left. Heartbroken. Pride intact.

But I didn't stop.

I found another agency—one that respected me. I booked small jobs. I pushed forward. Then came the call: I had been selected to assist Tina Turner at her Wildest Dreams Tour in Hartford.

Tina Turner. The legend.

I couldn't believe it until I was standing backstage, watching her electrify the stage, feeling the floor shake with the sound of her voice.

She turned to me afterward and smiled. "You did great."

Three words. A lifetime of encouragement.

In that moment, I felt it: I belonged in the room even if fear had almost kept me out of it.

The fear of failure doesn't just show up once. It creeps in again and again—when I started a business with my daughter, when I made my first sale at a pop-up market, when I watched that same business hurdle and eventually slow to a stop.

But every time fear came knocking, I answered with effort. With trying. By showing up.

Even greats like Stephen King felt that fear. Living in a trailer. Bills unpaid. Rejections stacked higher than his hopes. He once threw *Carrie*, his first novel, into the trash.

His wife pulled it back out. That story changed his life.

So, what do you do with feelings of unease? You don't let it win.

You don't wait for confidence to show up—you act first. Confidence comes later. You try, fail, try again. You start where you are—not where you wish you were. And if you fall? You learn. You rise. You keep going. Because success doesn't begin with luck, money, or perfection.

It begins with a choice.

Chapter 2: WHEN SELF-DOUBT WHISPERS

Self-doubt is that quiet, persistent voice in your head questioning your worth, your choices, and your ability to succeed. Sometimes it whispers just before you try something new. Other times, it hits like a storm that paralyzes progress. Everyone experiences it—but when it lingers, it can steal confidence, stall momentum, and cloud your vision of what's possible.

The Roots of Self-Doubt

Self-doubt doesn't appear without cause. Often, it begins in childhood—from harsh criticism, constant comparisons, or being made to feel invisible. A child told, *"You're not good enough,"* carries that wound into adulthood, still second-guessing every step.

Bullying, trauma, or repeated disappointments only deepen the cracks. When you've failed a test, lost a job, or watched a dream crumble, it's easy to believe you don't have what it takes. And when society bombards you with unrealistic standards of success, beauty, and achievement, you start feeling like you're behind—even when you're doing your best.

When Self-Criticism Becomes a Wall

I know this battle well.

Returning to school as an adult, I walked into the classroom with hope—until I got a "C" on a paper I worked hard on. Surrounded by younger classmates, I questioned everything: *Did I wait too long? Am I in over my head?*

At the same time, I launched Natural Essences LLC., a business rooted in my passion for healing. But weeks passed without a single sale. The silence was loud. Doubt crept in: *Was I dreaming too big? Am I cut out for this?*

That's how self-doubt works—it doesn't just appear during failure. It shows up in the pause before you begin, in the quiet moments when no one claps, and in the tension between where you are and where you want to be.

But growth is never comfortable, and success never arrives in a straight line. What I've learned is this: doubt loses power when you take action despite it.

Maya's Moment

Maya had big dreams: launching a wellness brand, speaking to audiences, and empowering women. Yet each time she moved forward, fear disguised as logic pulled her back: *"You're not ready. You're not good enough."*

She called it her invisible cage. No bars, just hesitation.

One evening, she watched a TED Talk where the speaker said: *"The only difference between those who make it and those who don't… is belief."* That line broke something open. Maya didn't wait to feel brave—she chose to move anyway.

Her first workshop had just five women. But they left changed. That was enough.

With each step forward, her questioning weakened—not because it vanished, but because she no longer let it lead.

Maya didn't become fearless. She became willing. And that's what truly matters.

The Power of Persistence: My YouTube Journey

When my husband and I started our YouTube channel, Studio Seven O, we were filled with energy and ideas. Each episode was a labor of love — hours of scripting, filming, editing, and reshooting. Then came a thrilling promotion. Suddenly, thousands of people were watching. It felt electric.

But when the promotion ended, so did the views. They plummeted to just forty per episode. The crushing silence made us question everything. Was all our effort wasted? Was the dream out of reach?

I'll never forget the day I attended the conference in Connecticut and saw Gabby Douglas speak. It wasn't just a typical keynote. It was raw, honest, and deeply human. She talked about lack of confidence—not from the outside looking in, but from the middle of it. And that stuck with me.

She spoke about training at Excalibur Gymnastics, discussing the intense pressure, the sacrifices, and the heavy expenses of chasing greatness. She talked about her coach, Liang Chow, and the relentless hours of practice. But more than anything, she shared the emotional side—the Lack of confidence, fear, the times when quitting probably felt easier than continuing.

Yet, despite all that, Gabby Douglas made history. In 2012, she became the first African American gymnast to win the Olympic all-around gold medal. That wasn't just a win—it was a message. A message that resilience, even when it feels invisible, matters. A message that self-doubt doesn't have to define you.

That day, I didn't just hear a motivational speech—I stole courage.

I tucked away her words for the days when I needed them most, like when my husband and I launched our YouTube channel, *Studio Seven O*, full of dreams but faced with crushing silence after the views dropped. Or when I sat in front of SHRM (Society for Human Resource Management) study materials, overwhelmed, knowing I'd only studied 4 hours that week instead of 20 hours. Or even in the quiet moments when I questioned if anything I was doing mattered at all.

That's when Gabby's voice came back to me. That's when I remembered: even Olympians have doubts. Even champions struggle. But they keep going.

Gabby taught me that courage doesn't mean never being afraid—it means doing it anyway. It means showing up, again and again, even when the crowd is gone and the applause has faded. It means believing in your future self enough to keep moving.

So now, when uncertainty about oneself creeps in, I remind myself: I've seen someone overcome it. I've heard her story. And if she can rise under the weight of the world, I can take another step too.

We all have our Olympics. They might not come with gold medals or global stages. But they come with meaning. They come with growth, and sometimes, they begin the moment we decide to believe, just like Gabby did.

The Bamboo Tree Lesson

Success is often invisible at first, like the Chinese bamboo tree. For five years, you water the seed and see no sign of growth. But underground, roots spread wide and deep. Then, suddenly, the tree shoots up 90 feet in six weeks. It didn't grow overnight — it grew silently, steadily.

Our journey with Studio Seven O is like that of a bamboo tree. Every episode, every late night, every setback is part of building a foundation strong enough to support something amazing. Even if progress isn't visible, it's happening.

The Journey to True Self-Esteem

Self-esteem isn't about perfection — it's about knowing, deep down, that you are enough. Not because of your appearance, achievements, or approval from others, but because you choose to believe in your own worth. It's the quiet strength to treat yourself with kindness, especially when the world doesn't.

I wasn't always confident. In school, I was teased for being "too skinny" and quiet. Those words stuck with me, like stones chipping away at my confidence. But then came Shannon — a friend whose kindness and laughter became a lifeline. Her support reminded me how powerful words can be: they can wound, or they can heal.

At home, where chaos often ruled, I found peace in books that spoke of confidence, purpose, and self-worth. Slowly, I realized that anyone else's judgment didn't define my value. I didn't need to change who I was to be worthy of love or success. I only needed to stop comparing myself and start owning my story.

You Are Enough — Without the Filter

In today's world of filters and highlight reels, it's easy to feel "less than." Social media platforms like Instagram and TikTok showcase perfection — flawless skin, luxury lifestyles, sculpted bodies, and seemingly effortless success. But behind every polished post is a carefully curated image that rarely reflects reality.

Jonathan Haidt stated, "Teens are particularly vulnerable to insecurity because their bodies and their social lives are changing so rapidly as they leave childhood. You can see the power of filters and tuning, as Instagram influencer Josephine Livin demonstrates how easy it is to essentially turn a dial and morph oneself into an increasingly unrealistic Instagram beauty. These turning apps give girls the ability to present themselves with perfect skin, fuller lips, bigger eyes, and a narrower waist."[1]

What starts as entertainment can slowly erode self-worth. You scroll through your feed and suddenly feel inadequate — like you don't measure up. You wonder why your skin isn't that clear, your life isn't that exciting, or your success isn't viral.

This constant comparison breeds self-doubt. You might start thinking:

- "If I'm not getting likes, I'm not good enough."
- "If I'm not trending, I must not be interesting."
- "If I'm not perfect, I won't be accepted."

Over time, this need for validation becomes addictive. And the more you seek approval online, the more you disconnect from your authentic, unfiltered self.

But here's the truth: you don't need likes to be lovable. You don't need to trend to have worth. You are not behind. You are on your own path — and that's your power.

Chapter 3: SHATTER THE CEILING: REWRITING YOUR BELIEFS

I often hear people talk about their past as if it's a life sentence. "They grew up wealthy," "Their dad was an engineer," or "Their parents left them with a house and a head start." These statements carry an unspoken message: *That's why they made it — and that's why I can't.* This is the invisible power of limiting beliefs—deeply ingrained thoughts that quietly dictate what we dare to dream, try, or believe about ourselves. They don't usually come from facts but from fear, comparison, and conditioning. Most people don't even realize they're living inside these mental cages. Limiting beliefs are false assumptions we accept as truth, often formed in childhood.

They whisper things like: "I'm not smart enough to run a business." "People like me don't get rich." "If I try and fail, I'll look like a fool." "Success is only for the lucky or privileged." These beliefs disguise themselves as logic or realism, but really, they are mental shortcuts designed to keep us safe — safe from risk, effort, and growth. For many, limiting beliefs start early. Growing up without financial security can teach us that struggle is the norm. Maybe you never saw entrepreneurs in your family or community, so success feels out of reach. Maybe when you voiced a big goal, you were told to "be realistic," and now ambition feels foolish.

Then there's the comparison trap. Seeing others with connections, inheritances, or privileged backgrounds, it's easy to say, "They had a head start. I never will." But while those advantages exist, believing you're doomed without them is a lie. The real danger? Limiting beliefs become self-fulfilling prophecies. If you believe you can't start a business because you didn't go to college, you won't try. If you think wealth is for "other people," you'll never learn how to create it. The truth is, success isn't reserved for a select few. It starts with a mindset that says: *Even if I start from nothing, I can still build something.*

For years, I carried a quiet but heavy belief: *I'm not where I want to be because no one showed me how.* I dreamed of being a talk show host or a YouTuber—who sparks meaningful conversations and connects people through stories. But every time I tried to move forward, I felt stuck. I blamed my parents for not teaching me the right skills. I blamed teachers for not encouraging me. I blamed the lack of mentors or connections. In my mind, if only someone had believed in me, I'd be further along. That belief felt justified. But it was a limiting belief — and it was costing me my future. Blaming others is like staring out a window, wishing the view would change. Growth doesn't happen through the window. It starts in the mirror.

One day, I finally looked in that mirror and asked: *What if the breakthrough starts with me?* That moment changed everything. Taking responsibility was freedom. When I stopped blaming others, I took back my power. No one else was coming to save me — and that wasn't bad news. It was an invitation to save myself.

How to Break Free from Limiting Beliefs

- **Notice them:** Where did this belief come from? Is it true?

- **Test the limits:** Take action even when afraid.

- **Surround yourself:** Find people who believe in growth.

- **Replace them:** Swap "I can't" for "I may not have started perfectly, but I have what I need to begin."

Your past shapes you, but doesn't define you. Your mindset, your actions, and your courage do.

Start where you are. Your dream isn't waiting for permission — it's waiting for you.

Real-Life Proof: Tyler Perry, Michael Phelps, and Howard Shultz

Take Tyler Perry, for example. Once homeless, now running a studio empire. He could've blamed the world, but he chose ownership over excuses. That choice transformed his life.

Howard Schultz — the man who built Starbucks into a global brand. Raised in Brooklyn's housing projects, Schultz knew struggle firsthand. His family lived paycheck to paycheck. His role models weren't CEOs; they were people doing their best to survive.

Yet Schultz didn't let his upbringing define him. He saw beyond the scarcity mindset, chose belief over limitation, and built a billion-dollar legacy.

Michael Phelps: The Power of Daily Habits Training -

- Context: The Olympic swimmer committed to six hours of training, six days a week, for years.

- Key Habits: Relentless practice, incremental improvement, and discipline.

- Breakthroughs: 28 Olympic medals show how daily discipline—more than occasional bursts of effort—creates world-class results.

Behind the Scenes: My Journey at Nutmeg TV

After college, I landed a part-time job at Nutmeg TV. It was minimum wage, nothing glamorous, but it sparked something inside me.

Walking into that TV studio, surrounded by cameras and creative minds, I felt both excitement and disbelief. "What am I doing here?" the voice whispered. I wasn't trained in media. I had no connections.

But I showed up. Day after day. Being in that space lit a fire. I stopped blaming and started building. It wasn't perfect, but it was real. I found my voice, my rhythm, and my purpose.

Soon, I launched my first show, *Building Relationships*, where guests shared stories of connection and strength. It was exactly what I imagined — honest, heartfelt, and mine.

The Power of Self-Awareness

For years, I thought I was doing everything right — working hard, chasing every opportunity. Yet, success felt just out of reach. I blamed circumstances, people, and lack of support.

Then I asked myself a tough question: *What if the biggest obstacle isn't out there — but inside me?*

This was the start of self-awareness — the practice of looking honestly at my habits, excuses, and patterns. I journaled. I asked:

- Why do I procrastinate on what matters?

- Why do I say yes to distractions but no to goals?

- Why do I wait for perfect conditions that never come?

I saw how I'd start strong but quit when it got hard. I avoided networking because I didn't feel "ready." I realized external roadblocks were real, but I'd let them become full stops instead of commas in my story.

Self-awareness gave me power. I wasn't my thoughts, but I was responsible for them. Ownership led to growth.

Chapter 4: THE POWER OF A CHANGED MIND

Napoleon Hill's timeless principle—*"Whatever the mind can conceive and believe, it can achieve"*—is more than motivational. It's a blueprint. But belief alone isn't enough. Hill also emphasized the power of daily discipline, definite purpose, and persistence. In *Your Success Routine*, we take that same foundation and put it into motion— Cognitive breakthrough showing how success is built not in leaps, but in the small, consistent habits that align with your vision. Belief is the spark. Routine is the engine.[1].

Success doesn't start with a paycheck, a title, or even talent—it starts with mind renewal.

Before the promotions, degrees, or recognition, there is an inner shift. One that begins not in what the world sees, but in what you begin to believe. Mindset transformation is that quiet but powerful turning point. It's the moment you stop asking for permission to grow and start giving yourself the authority to rise.

It's when *"I can't"* becomes *"I can learn."* When *"I'm stuck"* turns into *"I'm growing."* When your past stops being a life sentence and becomes the raw material for the future you're building.

---

[1] *Napoleon Hill, Think and Grow Rich*, 1937, p. 67

Way of thinking is not surface-level change—it's a profound, intentional rewiring of how you see yourself, your potential, and the world around you. It means challenging the limiting beliefs you've carried, the stories you've told yourself about what's possible, and the fear that's tried to keep you small. It's recognizing that growth isn't just for the chosen few—it's for those willing to select it, day after day.

So, what does this transformation really look like?

It's not accidental. It's deliberate. It's uncomfortable. And it's necessary.

You begin by examining the beliefs that have shaped your decisions, beliefs inherited from childhood, culture, failure, and fear. You tear down old mental models and construct new ones based on possibility, not limitation. You stop seeing change as something to dread and start seeing it as your greatest opportunity.

A transformed mindset affects every part of you. It doesn't just change how you think—it changes how you feel, how you show up, how you lead, and how you love. It unlocks resilience, ignites creativity, and rewires your response to obstacles.

It doesn't ignore reality—it redefines it.

Take Oprah Winfrey, for example.

Born into poverty in rural Mississippi, Oprah faced trauma, instability, and rejection. By every statistic, she should have been invisible. She could have internalized the message: *"Life has dealt me a bad hand, and that's that."* But she didn't.

Instead, she rewrote the script. She shifted from survival mode to a mission of purpose. From silence to a powerful voice. From limitation to legacy.

She embraced education, sharpened her communication, and viewed every hardship as fuel, not failure. The media industry didn't have a mold for someone like her, but Oprah wasn't trying to fit a mold—she was building something new. Her Frame of mentality said, *"There's power in authenticity,"* and the world leaned in to listen.

Today, Oprah isn't just a billionaire or a media icon. She's living proof of what happens when you stop playing small and start thinking differently.

But here's the truth—mindset transformation isn't reserved for public figures or high achievers. It's for anyone tired of the cycle they're in. Anyone ready to replace procrastination with action? Anyone willing to believe that the person they imagine becoming is not a fantasy—it's a version of them that's already waiting to be activated.

Maybe that's you.

Maybe your goal isn't fame—it's finally launching that YouTube channel, going back to school, writing your book, or chasing the dream that's been whispering to you for years.

Success doesn't wait for you to be fearless. It waits for you to say, "I'm ready to grow."

And your transformation? It might just be the spark someone else needs to begin their own.

Let me tell you about mine.

When I set the goal to pass the SHRM (Society for Human Resource Management) certification exam, it wasn't just about adding a credential to my résumé. This wasn't just a test—it was a turning point. A gateway into a higher level of mastery in human resources. SHRM is rigorous, preparing professionals for the real-world complexities of HR. I knew passing it would position me for new opportunities. But knowing and doing? Those are two very different things.

The first two weeks of my so-called "study plan" were a mess.

I'd set the alarm early, determined to get ahead. But when it rang? Snooze. Over and over. After work, I had every intention of studying—but instead, I found myself strolling through the mall, shopping for things I didn't need. At night, I'd sit down with my study materials... and turn on *POWER* instead. "Just one episode," I'd tell myself. You know how that goes. One turned into three, and somehow, I was on the phone, laughing, chatting like I didn't have a goal breathing down my neck.

My SHRM (Society for Human Resource Management) books sat unopened on the table—reminders of a commitment I wasn't keeping. I felt guilty. I felt uneasy. But more than anything, I felt overwhelmed. The truth? I wasn't lazy—I was scared. I didn't believe I had what it took, and my perspective reflected that.

I told myself I'd study 22.5 hours a week, on top of my full-time job. Ambitious, right? That first week, I managed four: the next, maybe five. I fell behind. But I didn't quit. Instead, I decided to change what mattered most—how I thought about it.

I didn't need a better plan. I needed a better thinking pattern.

So, I decided to do something different. I sat down, cleared my desk, and created a calendar—not just any calendar, but a *routine roadmap* to focus.

It wasn't perfect. I blocked out time to study, cook, help kids, etc.

Time	Activity
5:00 AM – 6:30 AM	Study SHRM (Morning Session)
6:30 AM – 8:00 AM	Get dressed & prep for work
8:00 AM – 8:30 AM	Commute to work
8:30 AM – 4:30 PM	Work hours
4:30 PM – 5:00 PM	Commute home
5:00 PM – 5:30 PM	Wind down / prep to cook
5:30 PM – 6:30 PM	Cook dinner
6:30 PM – 7:00 PM	Eat dinner
7:10 PM – 7:35 PM	Clean up
7:35 PM – 8:15 PM	Help kids until bedtime
8:30 PM – 9:30 PM	Study SHRM (Evening Session)

Total SHRM Study Time per Weekday: 2.5 hours **Total SHRM Study (Mon–Fri)**: 12.5 hours

Saturday

Time	Activity
Morning–3:00 PM	Free time / errands / family
3:00 PM – 8:00 PM	Study SHRM (5-hour session)
Evening	Relax / prep for Sunday

Sunday

Time	Activity
Morning–3:00 PM	Free time / rest / family
3:00 PM – 8:00 PM	Study SHRM (5-hour session)
Evening	Wind down / prep for week

Total SHRM Study Time (Weekend): 5 hours/day × 2 = **10 hours/week**

Instead of shaming myself for the hours I missed, I celebrated the ones I showed up for. I surrounded myself with positivity—uplifting podcasts, sticky notes filled with affirmations, and my daughter's encouragement." Mom, you can do it." Her belief in me, especially on the days I doubted, became my fuel.

Each week, I did a little more. I felt a shift—not just in my habits, but in my thinking. I replaced guilt with gratitude. I reminded myself that growth is messy and that progress, no matter how slow, still counts.

Sure, there were still slips. Days when I chose comfort over discipline. But this time, I didn't spiral. I just restarted. Again and again.

Because positivity isn't magic—it's mindset. A better viewpoint gives you the power to keep going.

Hour by hour, chapter by chapter, I rebuild my confidence. I mastered the material. And when I finally sat down to take that test, I wasn't just prepared—I was transformed.

Passing the SHRM exam wasn't just a professional win—it was a personal revolution.

Yes, I got certified. Yes, I eventually earned a position as Vice President of Human Resources. But the real victory? I became the kind of person who follows through. Who honors her goals. Who understands the power of structure, consistency, and self-discipline?

And I still carry that approach with me today—in every project, every decision, every season of growth.

So, let me ask you: what story are you telling yourself?

Because if you're waiting to feel ready, to have the perfect plan, to finally be unshakable —you'll be waiting forever.

Start now. Start small. Start scared. Just start.

Because triumph doesn't begin with the finish line, it begins the moment you believe you were built to cross it.

Mastering Spanish: From Beginner to Fluent

When I was in my teens, I remember hearing things that stuck with me for years, not because they were true, but because they were *loud*. Family members and even friends would say things like, *"You're just going to end up with a bunch of kids, living on Section 8."* Or, *"It's too late for you to go back to school."* And one that hurt more than I admitted at the time: *"You'll never learn Spanish—why even try?"*

Those words planted seeds of self-questioning, people's limiting beliefs that tried to grow with me. For a while, I let them. I repeated those same lines to myself. *Maybe they're right. Maybe I missed my window. Maybe I'm not meant for more.*

But something in me refused to let those beliefs be the end of my story.

At some point, I realized: those weren't my thoughts. They were echoes of someone else's fears, someone else's limitations. And I had a choice. I could either let those voices define me—or rewrite the narrative.

So I started changing the conversation in my mind. I already knew the formula of good habits and how to revamp my perspective.

I began replacing every limiting belief with an empowering affirmation:

"I'm not too late—I'm right on time for my purpose."
"I can learn anything I set my mind to."

"Other people's expectations will not define my life."

"Other people's expectations will not define my life."

"They may be talking about themselves, but they are definitely not talking about Cha Roc."

And then I took action. My daily routines were every morning and evening (5–30 minutes) – *I started with exposure.*

- Listen to Spanish audio while getting ready (podcast, YouTube, or Spotify playlist).

Examples: "Coffee Break Spanish," "Duolingo Podcast," or "Notes in Spanish."

- Read a Spanish sentence or two from an app like Duolingo, Babbel, Spanish movies, or a Spanish quote site. Repeat aloud: Practice pronunciation, even if it feels silly. Speaking wakes up your brain.

I walked the streets of Puerto Rico, danced in Mexico, soaked in the sun of the Dominican Republic, and explored the beauty of Costa Rica more than once. I made it my mission not just to speak the language, but to *live* it. I'd learned that with a different growth outlook, *anything* is possible.

I joined a group of people I met online, all of us on a mission to learn Spanish and immerse ourselves in the culture. That mission brought us to Málaga, a coastal gem in southern Spain. It was more than just a language trip—it was a life-changing experience.

Málaga is a city where the past and present coexist in perfect harmony. The sea sparkles with promise. The streets hum with energy. And the people—warm, expressive, and full of life—welcomed me like I was family.

One of the most unforgettable places was the Alcazaba of Málaga—an 11th-century Moorish fortress perched on a hill. Its terraced gardens, delicate fountains, and panoramic views of the city and sea took my breath away. I wasn't just seeing Spain; I was being introduced to its soul—its history, its rhythm, its artistry.

What started as a simple goal to learn a language evolved into something much more. I fell in love—not just with Spanish, but with the entire culture. The food, the music, the late-night conversations that stretched into the early morning, the kindness of strangers who became friends.

I've returned to Málaga three times since that first trip. And every time, I discover something new—not just about the city, but about myself. Not because it was easy. But because I build positive routines and stay committed. Every trip, every conversation in Spanish, every class I completed was a silent "I told you so"—not to those who second-guessed me, but to the voice inside that once believed them.

The Invisible Switch

There was a time when I believed success was reserved for "other people"—the confident, the polished, those who always seemed to know what they were doing. I'd watch them lead, create, or speak and quietly think, I could never do that.

But that belief wasn't based on fact. It came from fear—a fixed mindset, the idea that abilities are set in stone, that you either have "it" or you don't. I didn't realize how much this empowerment lens was shaping my choices, keeping me in my comfort zone and making me second-guess myself, always waiting for the perfect moment to act.

Then, one day, something shifted.

At a workshop, I listened to a speaker explain the difference between a fixed and a growth mindset, also known as a champion mentality. They said, "A fixed perspective says, 'I'm not good at this.' A growth mindset says, 'I'm not good at this…yet.'" That one word—yet—hit me like a wave.

In that moment, I understood: Abundance perspective isn't just how you think; it's how you see yourself.

I began to experiment. Instead of saying, "I'm not good on camera," I tried, "I'm learning to be confident on camera." I shifted from "I've never done this before" to "This is a chance to grow." Every time my inner critic appeared, I reminded myself: I am a work in progress, not behind.

That small shift changed everything.

Suddenly, I was willing to try more, to fail forward, to say yes to opportunities I would have avoided. I stopped asking, "Am I ready?" Instead, I asked, "Am I willing?"

And I was.

That's the true power of mindset. It's not a magic fix, but it is the invisible switch that moves you from stuck to unstoppable.

Think about it: Michael Jordan was cut from his high school team but came back stronger. J.K. Rowling faced rejection after rejection before publishing Harry Potter. Countless others have gone from doubting their dreams to building them—one decision at a time.

Ask yourself: What if the biggest thing standing between you and the life you want is simply the story you keep telling yourself?

How a Mindset Shift Truly Happens

Carol S. Dweck, a pioneering psychologist and professor at Stanford University, has revolutionized our understanding of human potential through her research on mindset. Her work reveals that the way we perceive our abilities profoundly shapes our motivation, learning, and success.[2] Dweck's research demonstrates that cultivating a growth mindset can lead to higher achievement, greater creativity, and improved well-being.

Transforming your way of thinking isn't about one dramatic epiphany; it's about steadily flipping the internal switch from limitation to possibility. Here's how that transformation unfolds:

1. **Recognize Limiting Beliefs**
   Identify the thoughts that hold you back—those inner narratives whispering you're not capable or not enough.

2. **Challenge Old Assumptions**
   Ask: *Is this belief true? Does it help me grow?* Replace outdated assumptions with ones grounded in possibility and self-trust.

3. **Adopt a Growth Perspective**
   Believe you can develop your abilities and that opportunities outweigh limitations. This unlocks creativity, persistence, and confidence.

4. **Reinforce Through Action**
   Real change comes through consistent practice—set

---

[2] Dweck, 2006

goals, reflect, learn from setbacks, and keep moving forward.

5. **Build a Supportive Environment**
   Growth accelerates when you're both encouraged and challenged. Seek mentors, therapists, or communities that provide accountability.

6. **Set Clear Goals**
   Define exactly what you want and why. Clarity fuels motivation; vagueness stalls progress.

7. **Rewire Limiting Thoughts**
   If you catch yourself thinking *I can't*, pause and challenge it. Replace uncertainty with affirmations like *I am capable and growing*.

8. **Visualize Breakthrough**
   Picture yourself achieving your goal—*feel it, see it, live it.* Visualization primes your brain to create that reality.

Remember: You can choose your perspective. You can rewrite your story. The invisible switch is always within reach—flip it and set your life in motion.

Bending Without Breaking: Resilience and Adaptability

There's a moment we all face at some point in life—the moment when the plan falls apart. For me, it didn't come with fireworks or a dramatic crash. It came quietly, like a slow unraveling. A new opportunity, I thought, would change everything, but it didn't. A project I poured my heart into stalled. The momentum I had built started to fade. And there I was—tired, discouraged, and dangerously close to quitting. That's when I learned that resilience isn't about how strong you are when everything's going right. It's about how you respond when everything starts going wrong.

At first, I resisted. I kept replaying the missteps, analyzing the failures, wondering what I could've done differently. But the truth is, hurdles don't ask for our permission—and they rarely arrive when we're ready. What they do offer, though, is an invitation: to grow, to stretch, to adapt. So, I took a breath, and I chose to adapt.

I started by letting go of how I thought things were supposed to go. I stopped clinging to perfection and started focusing on progress. I permitted myself to feel the frustration—but I didn't set up camp there.

Instead, I asked, "What can I learn? What can I change? How can I keep going, even if it looks different from what I imagined?"

That's when I found my resilience.

It wasn't flashy. It didn't always feel brave. However, it appeared when I adjusted my routine to accommodate the new circumstances. It showed up when I tried again after a public failure. It showed up every time I said, "I'll figure it out," instead of "I'm done." And slowly, things began to shift. Not magically—but *meaningfully.*

Resilience taught me to stay grounded when things got hard. Adaptability taught me to pivot instead of panic. Together, they built something stronger than confidence: mental toughness—the kind that carries you through stormy seasons with your head held high, even when your heart is heavy.

Think about a tree during a storm. The rigid ones? They snap. The flexible ones? They bend. That's what resilience looks like. It's not about standing still in the wind. It's about swaying with it and still standing when the sky clears.

History is full of people who built breakthroughs on resilience. Take Nelson Mandela, who spent 27 years in prison and emerged not bitter, but ready to lead. Or Bethany Hamilton, who lost her arm to a shark attack and returned to surfing. Or even countless everyday people—teachers, single parents, small business owners—who rise every day against odds most never see.

Their secret isn't luck. It's that they refused to let setbacks define them. So, if you're facing roadblocks right now—if the plan has unraveled and you're wondering what's next—remember this: Resilience doesn't mean you never fall. It means you rise every single time. Adaptability doesn't mean you give up on your dream.

It means you find a new way to reach it. And Resilience? That's just the quiet strength inside you that says, "I'm not done yet." Resilience is the quiet strength inside you that refuses to give up. It's what allows you to stand back up after a fall, even when your heart is heavy or your confidence shaken.

Adaptability is your ability to adjust, to pivot, to keep moving even when the road ahead looks different from what you imagined. It's being open to new paths, new solutions, and new identities.

It's when life says, *"No,"* and you answer, *"Okay, what's next?"*

When you adapt, you let go of rigid expectations and allow yourself to evolve.
You stop resisting the change and start using it.

Adaptable people don't just survive—they learn how to thrive in any situation. There was a season in my life when everything I had carefully built began to fall apart. The day my job shut down is still etched in my memory." My savings disappeared faster than I imagined. A relationship I thought was forever ended with no warning. I remember sitting on my bed in silence, staring at the wall, numb.

My thoughts felt like quicksand—every time I tried to stand, I sank deeper.

It was tempting to give up. To let life happen *to* me instead of pushing back.
But something in me—small, but stubborn—refused to stay down.

That's when I learned the true meaning of resilience. It's not about being unaffected by the storm. It's about standing *anyway*—even when the wind won't let you breathe.

I started small. I permitted myself to feel, but not to stay stuck.

I replaced "Why me?" with "What can I learn from this?"

I stopped waiting for the perfect opportunity and adapted to what I had. I took freelance gigs. Learned new skills online. Took walks when I couldn't afford therapy. Read books that reminded me I wasn't alone.

Most of all, I redefined what failure means. It wasn't the end. It was a chapter. A painful one, yes—but also a powerful one. I began to see obstacles not as walls, but as detours—unwanted, but sometimes necessary to lead you where you're truly meant to go.

That's adaptability—the ability to shift, to bend without breaking. It's learning to dance in the rain instead of waiting for the storm to pass. Months later, I found a new job that allowed me to do work I loved. My confidence grew. I was no longer who I was before the storm—I was stronger, sharper, and far more grateful.

Reactive Language and Proactive Language

Understanding the difference between reactive and proactive language is crucial for achieving your goals. The way you speak—especially to yourself—shapes your actions and determines your outcomes.

Reactive language reflects a victim's way of thinking, placing control outside oneself: on other people, circumstances, or luck. Proactive language, on the other hand, reflects a leadership mindset. It hands control back to you, empowering you to take initiative and responsibility.

Reactive Language	Proactive Language
"I can't."	"How can I?"
"That's just the way I am."	"I can improve."
"There's nothing I can do."	"I'll find a solution."

What I Learned from "The Pursuit of Happyness"

When I first watched *The Pursuit of Happyness*, it was based on a true story. I expected just a movie, but I got a lesson in persistence and the power of proactive language. Chris Gardner, played by Will Smith, faces extreme hardships—broke, homeless, raising a young son. Gardner refuses to give up on his dreams. Through resilience, determination, and unwavering dedication to his son, he earns an unpaid internship at a prestigious brokerage firm, eventually transforming his life and achieving professional and personal success. The film emphasizes perseverance, hope, and the power of never giving up, even in the face of overwhelming obstacles. He could have fallen back on reactive language: "It's not fair," or "There's nothing I can do." That would have given his power away.

Instead, Chris embodied proactive language—not just through what he said, but how he lived. When he declared, "I'm going to be a stockbroker," people laughed, but he never said, "If I get lucky." He said, "I'm going to…" claiming ownership over his future.

Even during his lowest moments, Chris spoke and acted with resolve, never pity. Whenever life pushed back, he responded, "Then I'll find another way."

One scene stayed with me: Chris tells his son, *"Don't ever let somebody tell you you can't do something. Not even me. You got a dream, you gotta protect it."*

That wasn't just advice for his son—it was a reminder for me: our words shape our future.

After seeing the movie, I changed how I talked to myself:

- No more "I can't."
- No more "Maybe someday."
- I started saying, "I will." "I choose to." "This is hard, but I've got this."

If Chris Gardner could stay proactive through the worst of times, so can I.

Malala Yousafzai: A Voice That Refused to Be Silenced

Malala Yousafzai was born in Mingora, Pakistan, in 1997, in the beautiful but often troubled Swat Valley. Her father was a teacher and a passionate advocate for education. From a young age, Malala had a passion for learning. She dreamed of becoming a doctor and was often at the top of her class.

But as the Taliban began to take control of her region, everything changed.

Girls were banned from attending school. Schools were bombed. Education—especially for girls—was under attack.

Most children were afraid to speak out. But not Malala.

At just 11 years old, she began writing a secret blog for the BBC under a pseudonym, describing life under Taliban rule and her fight to keep learning. Her voice was clear, honest, and brave.

But her activism made her a target.

On October 9, 2012, Malala was just 15 when a Taliban gunman boarded her school bus and shot her in the head. The bullet traveled through her head, neck, and shoulder. Many believed she wouldn't survive.

But Malala lived. And not only did she survive—she came back stronger. After surviving the Taliban's attack, instead of saying "They silenced me" (reactive), she said They thought that the bullets would silence us, but they failed. This proactive statement shifts the focus from what was done to her to how she chooses to respond—with courage and resilience.

In 2014, at just 17 years old, Malala became the youngest-ever Nobel Peace Prize winner.

Persistence and Willpower: The Unstoppable Force Behind Success

Success isn't just about talent, intelligence, or being in the right place at the right time. Those things help, but they're not the whole story. The real game-changer is determination — the combination of persistence and willpower that refuses to quit when things get tough.

Persistence is what keeps you moving when the road is long, the results are slow, and the failures are piling up. It's not about perfection; it's about progress. Thomas Edison didn't see thousands of failed experiments as defeat — he saw them as steps toward the lightbulb. That's the power of persistence: turning setbacks into stepping stones.

You see it in the student who studies harder after failing a test, the entrepreneur who launches again after a failed startup, the athlete who trains even harder after a loss. They know the truth: big goals don't happen overnight — they're earned through consistent effort and unwavering resolve.

Willpower is the other half of the equation. It's the inner muscle that resists the easy option in favor of the right one. Walter Mischel's marshmallow experiment proved it — Children who were able to wait—demonstrating stronger self-control—tended to have better outcomes later in life, such as higher academic achievement, stronger social skills, and better emotional regulation. Essentially, the ability to delay gratification early on predicted greater long-term success because these children could resist short-term temptations in favor of more meaningful rewards in the future. Walter Mischel's marshmallow experiment is a classic study:

- Participants: Preschool children at Stanford University.

- Procedure: Each child was given a choice: eat one marshmallow immediately or wait a short period to receive two marshmallows.

- Findings: Children who were able to wait for the second marshmallow generally showed better outcomes later in life, including higher academic achievement, healthier relationships, and better coping skills.

- Conclusion: The ability to exercise willpower and delay gratification is a strong predictor of long-term success.

So, when you hear, "Willpower is the guardrail that keeps you on track…", it's directly tied to the idea that resisting temptation early can lead to greater rewards later.

Determination in Action

Multiple publishers rejected J.K. Rowling before Harry Potter became a global phenomenon. LeBron James rose from humble beginnings to become one of the greatest athletes in history. He has leveraged his platform for business ventures, philanthropy, and social activism, demonstrating that true success encompasses impact and influence that extend beyond personal achievements. What fueled them wasn't just skill — it was the relentless mix of persistence and willpower that turned "maybe" into "I did it."

The lesson? Talent can start the race, but determination wins it. When persistence keeps you moving and willpower keeps you focused, success stops being a possibility and becomes a promise.

Beyond that, devotion is not exclusive to famous individuals. It thrives in everyday people, single parents working multiple jobs to support their children, students overcoming learning difficulties, or immigrants building new lives in foreign countries. These stories may not always make headlines, but they represent the same core principle: unwavering dedication in the face of adversity.

While some people seem naturally determined, research suggests that persistence and willpower can be strengthened like muscles. Setting small, achievable goals and gradually increasing challenges builds confidence and resilience. Cultivating a growth mindset —the belief that abilities can be developed through effort —also reinforces the value of persistence.

Additionally, supportive environments play a vital role. Encouragement from mentors, peers, and family members can provide the motivation needed to keep going. Positive reinforcement and a sense of purpose fuel the fire of determination, especially during difficult times.

Chapter 5: CUTTING TIES

Prioritizing Success by Eliminating Negativity Pruning for Growth

There comes a moment when holding on does more damage than letting go. It's not just about preference—it's about purpose. If you want to evolve, you'll have to make peace with the painful truth: not everyone can go where you're headed.

Success isn't just built on hard work or talent. Your environment shapes it—the energy around you, the voices in your ear, the attitudes you absorb. Certain people uplift and energize you; others slowly diminish your strength.

And one of the most powerful decisions you'll ever make is choosing who gets access to your vision.

Letting go isn't abandonment. It's alignment.

We don't outgrow people because we're better than them. We outgrow them because our dreams require more than their comfort zone can handle. Like a gardener pruning branches to help a tree bear fruit, we must cut back on what no longer feeds our future.

Rooted in Nature, Built with Love

When I launched my natural oils and handmade soap business, I was electric with excitement. My mind swirled with ideas—scents, packaging, pop-up markets. I imagined my friends cheering me on. But reality hits differently.

"You're selling what?" Jenna raised an eyebrow, squinting at the sample in her hand.

"Oils and soaps. All organic, handcrafted," I said with a hopeful smile.

She smirked. "Why would I buy this when I can get soap from Family Dollar?"

Her friend laughed. I forced a chuckle, too, but inside, I felt the sting.

Over the next few weeks, every mention of my business was met with sarcasm or silence. Their doubts seeped into my spirit. I found myself shrinking, censoring my excitement to avoid judgment.

Until one night, clarity hit me like a lightning bolt: Support doesn't always come with understanding, but it must come with respect.

I was investing energy in people who didn't believe in me. That had to stop.

There was no dramatic farewell—just a quiet exit. I stopped sharing my dreams with those who mocked them. I stepped back from the group chats and leaned into new spaces—online communities for small business owners, craft fairs, and entrepreneurs. There, I found connection, encouragement, and even my first customers.

"Letting go" hurt. But staying would've hurt more.

The shift wasn't just emotional. It was transformational. I stopped needing approval and started building momentum. My business began to thrive—not only because of strategy or hustle, but because I finally stood in soil that allowed me to grow.

You can't thrive in toxic ground.

People talk about the "crabs in a barrel" mindset—where one person tries to climb, and the others pull them back down. I lived it. Their fear, their jealousy, their limitations had nothing to do with me—until I let them define me.

Cutting ties isn't cruelty. It's clarity. It's choosing purpose over the past. Peace over popularity. Vision over validation.

If you're on the verge of something bold, and the people around you only offer doubt, it's time to ask yourself: *Are they fueling your fire—or putting it out?*

You don't have to make a scene. You have to make a decision.

Because sometimes, the boldest step toward success is pruning what no longer blooms.

Letting Go of Toxic Friendships to Protect Your Success

There comes a time when you must evaluate the people around you—not from a place of judgment, but from clarity. Some friendships uplift and energize you; others subtly undermine your confidence and progress. Toxic relationships don't always come with loud conflict—sometimes they show up as quiet dismissal, constant criticism, or one-sided loyalty.

Start by reflecting on how certain connections make you feel. Do they inspire you or exhaust you? Do they encourage your development and growth, or make you second-guess your goals? Recognizing these patterns is the first step to reclaiming your energy and focus.

If the relationship feels safe enough, have a calm, honest conversation. Let the other person know how you feel, without blame. If that's not possible—or you've already tried—begin creating distance. You don't need drama to walk away. A shift in your energy, attention, and time is often enough.

Grieving a friendship, even a toxic one, is normal. Writing a private goodbye letter can help you release unspoken feelings and process what you've learned. Forgiveness doesn't mean forgetting—it means freeing yours if from resentment so you can move forward in peace.

My friend Jasmin learned this the hard way. She was known for her support—always clapping, sharing, and cheering others on. "Support is free," she'd say. "It costs nothing to show love." But when she launched her own online shop, the energy wasn't returned. The same friends she had driven hours for, reposted for, and encouraged—said nothing.

At first, she felt hurt. Then foolish. But finally, she felt free.

"Real support doesn't have to be begged for," she told me. "Loyalty should never be one-sided."

She stopped pouring into people who didn't pour back. And when she found her real tribe—the ones who celebrated her without being asked—she never looked back.

This is why letting go matters.

By creating space, you make room for genuine connections. You reduce unnecessary stress and align your life with people who share your vision and values. Protecting your peace isn't selfish, it's essential for prosperity.

So, if you're clinging to relationships that leave you drained or doubting, ask yourself:
Are they building you up—or burning you out?

The choice isn't always easy. But it is powerful.

Sometimes, improvement begins the moment you stop explaining yourself and start honoring yourself.

The Three Styles: Givers, Takers, and Matchers

When cutting ties, remember the balance of relationships—givers uplift, takers drain, and matchers mirror; understanding who stands in each role helps you choose wisely who deserves space in your life. Grant (2013) explained that people operate as givers, takers, or matchers.

At a mid-sized tech company, a new product launch was underway. The team consisted of three key players: Crystal, Mike, and Nancy.

Crystal – The Giver

Crystal was always the first to offer help. Whether it was staying late to help a teammate debug code or mentoring new hires, she gave without keeping score. She genuinely believed that when one person wins, the whole team does.

During the product launch, she took on extra work to help the team meet a tight deadline—even finishing parts of Mike's assignment when he didn't follow through.

Mike– The Taker

Mike was smart and charismatic, but was always looking for ways to *maximize personal gain*. He frequently spoke in meetings and ensured his name was associated with the project's successful aspects. But behind the scenes, he often delegated his tasks or missed deadlines, expecting others (like Crystal) to clean up after him.

When the product launch succeeded, he made sure to take credit in front of upper management—even for things Crystal had done.

Nancy – The Matcher

Nancy was competent and fair. She helped people when they helped her. If someone stayed late to help her one day, she returned the favor the next. She wasn't as outwardly generous as Crystal, but also didn't let people take advantage of her like Mike tried to do.

When Nancy saw Crystal being overworked and Mike skating by, she pulled Crystal aside. "You've got to draw the line," she said. Then she subtly made it known to the manager how much Crystal had contributed and how little Mike had.

Eventually, the manager began noticing patterns. Crystal was praised and given a leadership opportunity—once she learned to set better boundaries and be a *smart giver*, not a *self-sacrificing one*. Mike's reputation began to catch up with him; colleagues were wary of working with him, and his influence shrank. Nancy remained respected and steady, playing her part and maintaining balance.

People are matchers by default, seeking to maintain a fair balance in their relationships.

Givers can be highly successful, but only if they avoid being exploited by takers. They are overrepresented among both the least and most successful people in organizations, depending on how they manage their giving.

Takers may achieve short-term gains but often struggle to maintain trust and long-term relationships. They may view interactions as opportunities to "get over" to exploit, outsmart, or come out ahead, regardless of fairness.

Reciprocity styles can shift depending on the context or role someone might play; for instance, they might be a giver with close friends, a matcher with colleagues, and a taker in negotiations.

Absolutely—when building a strong, loyal, and high-performing team, understanding whether someone is a Giver, Taker, or Matcher can be incredibly valuable. Here's how people can identify these types—and why loyalty is often found more in Givers and Matchers than in Takers.

How to Identify Givers, Takers, and Matchers?

- Givers: They offer help without being asked. Celebrate others' prosperity. Don't keep score.

  o Behavior in Teams: Build trust quickly. Often go the extra mile for the group. Show *quiet loyalty* over time. People often can spot a giver, and they can easily get taken advantage of.

  o Watch for: Risk of burnout if not supported or protected from Takers.

- Takers: They talk more about themselves than others. Take credit, avoid blame. Only offer help when it benefits them. They brag about projects or things they have accomplished, but it's generally with help. They embellish the truth.

- - Behavior in Teams - Create division, distrust; Appear charming or "star players" at first.

  - Watch for: Shallow loyalty—often tied to what they can gain. Other names for them include beggars and moochers. They will ask for money, and most of the time, they will not repay it.

- Matchers - signs will help if they see it as fair. They expect reciprocity and pay attention to balance.

  - Behavior in Teams - Act as stabilizers, call out injustice or freeloaders.

  - Watch for: They show loyalty when it's mutual.

The Courage to Choose Yourself

Personal growth isn't passive—it's a deliberate, often painful choice.

It begins the moment you stop asking for permission to evolve. The moment you stop shrinking yourself to fit into the stories others wrote for you. That's when you start choosing peace over performance. Dreams over duty. Wholeness over habit.

Cutting ties doesn't always look dramatic. Sometimes it's just a quiet moment of clarity—when you say, without apology: "I choose me."

But let's be honest—choosing yourself comes with grief. You'll second-guess your strength. You'll mourn the memories that felt like home. You'll sit in silence and wonder if the cost is too high.

And that's okay.

Grief is proof that your efforts matter. It echoes transformation, marking the space between who you were and who you are becoming. Because what comes next is nothing short of sacred.

You begin to hear your own voice more clearly. You start making choices that reflect your worth—not your wounds. You surround yourself with people who love you for who you are now, not just the role you used to play in their lives.

This is the courage to choose yourself. It's not loud. It's not easy.

But it's always worth it.

The Weight of the Thank You

Although difficult, it's often necessary to let go of someone you love. Saying Thank You or Love isn't always enough, especially when that love comes with manipulation, control, or emotional stagnation. Cutting ties doesn't mean you don't care; it means you care more about your well-being. Sometimes, the most loving thing you can do for both yourself and the other person is to create distance. Space creates clarity. Clarity is the first step toward new beginnings.

I know this guy in the neighborhood—his name's Malik. When Malik started his business, he had nothing but an idea, a beat-up laptop, and a dream bigger than his living room.

He worked 16-hour days, studied financial literacy at night, and failed more times than he cared to admit. But through the early grind, a few people stepped in to help. An aunt who sometimes mailed his orders. A cousin who washed dishes while he handled customer emails. A friend who'd say, "You got this," when he looked like he didn't.

Malik was grateful. Truly.

But then the business grew. He went from barely making rent to running payroll, from struggling to sell 10 items a week to shipping globally.

That's when the whispers started: *"He could at least buy me a house." "After everything I did, that's all I get?" "He's acting brand new now."*

The gratitude he once felt turned into guilt—and then into pressure. Because it was no longer about kindness, it was about expectations.

One day, Malik sat down and wrote in his journal:

"I will always appreciate those who helped me — but appreciation is not ownership. My success is not community property. I am not a lottery ticket. I'm not ungrateful—I'm just not responsible for rewriting everyone's life story."

He realized this truth:

Just because someone helped you during the struggle, doesn't mean they get to dictate how you move in success. Support should come without strings. And generosity should come from the heart, not guilt.

Some millionaires never bought their parents a house—not because they're selfish, but because relationships are complicated. Not every story is Instagram-perfect. Not every bond is deep. And no one—not even family—is entitled to your milestone.

Malik still gives donations. Still loves. Still remembers who was there.

But now he gives with wisdom—not pressure. Because in the end, success isn't a payment. It's a journey. And it belongs to the one who walked it.

Steve Jobs was an American entrepreneur, inventor, and business magnate best known as the co-founder of Apple Inc. He played a pivotal role in revolutionizing the personal computer, smartphone, music, and digital publishing industries. Steve Jobs initially denied paternity of his daughter, Lisa Brennan-Jobs, and provided limited support in her early life. Though they later reconnected, Lisa has spoken publicly about their complicated relationship and how emotionally distant he was even after becoming a billionaire.

Wealth doesn't erase family dysfunction. Jobs's case shows that success doesn't always lead to ideal personal relationships or financial support.

Eminem is an American rapper, songwriter, and record producer. He is widely regarded as one of the most influential and skilled hip-hop artists of all time. Eminem has been very open about his troubled relationship with his mother, Debbie Mathers. In his early career, he accused her of abuse and neglect. Despite his massive success, he distanced himself from her and didn't offer financial support for many years.

He protected his mental health and his daughter first. Family ties didn't override his personal trauma.

Chapter 6: BEFORE YOU CAN MOVE FORWARD, YOU MUST KNOW WHAT'S HOLDING YOU BACK

Before you can move past a challenge, you have to define it clearly. That may sound simple, but many people stay stuck because they're reacting to discomfort without understanding its root cause.

Why it matters:

You can't solve what you don't understand. When a problem remains vague—"I'm just overwhelmed" or "nothing's working"—you risk wasting energy on the symptoms instead of addressing the source. Clarity is the first step toward progress.

Action step:

Describe the barrier in specific terms. Is it lack of time, fear of failure, financial pressure, lack of knowledge, or comparison? Instead of saying, "I feel stuck," say, "I'm struggling to stay consistent because I'm exhausted after work." When you get honest and specific, you regain power over the situation.

Once the obstacle is named, you can start building strategies around it—rather than just reacting to it.

Challenges and Reframing Obstacles

One powerful technique is to shift your mindset: instead of seeing an obstacle as a dead end, view it as a problem to be solved. Asking "How can I overcome this?" rather than "Why is this happening to me?" builds resilience and sparks creative thinking.

Another strategy is to break big problems into smaller, actionable steps. Progress becomes more manageable—and less intimidating—when taken one step at a time.

Seeking input from mentors, coaches, or trusted peers can also bring clarity and insight. Their experience often uncovers solutions we might not see on our own. When we combine thought patterns, action, and support, barriers become stepping stones to meaningful progress.

Beyond the Clock: Defeating Time Management Barriers

When I worked at a company in New York City on Broadway, I often found myself struggling with tight deadlines. The fast-paced environment and constant flow of tasks made it easy to lose track of time. I realized that I was missing deadlines not because of a lack of effort, but because I struggled with managing my time effectively.

At first, I tried to multitask, bouncing between emails, meetings, and project work, but that only made things worse. Important tasks slipped through the cracks. One day, after missing a key deliverable for a client presentation, I knew something had to change.

So, I started to break the problem down:

The issue wasn't just about being "egregious at time management" — it was that I underestimated how long tasks would take, didn't set priorities clearly, and didn't block focused time in my day.

I decided to take practical steps:

1. I started using my calendar to schedule focused work sessions.

2. I set daily priorities each morning, limiting my list to 3 major tasks.

3. I started using the Pomodoro technique to stay on track and avoid burnout. The Pomodoro Technique is a time management method. It uses a simple system to boost focus and productivity by breaking work into intervals:

    - Work for 25 minutes (called one *Pomodoro*, Italian for "tomato," after the tomato-shaped kitchen timer that creators used.

    - Take a 5-minute break.

    - After completing four Pomodoros, take a longer break (15–30 minutes).

The idea is that short, focused bursts of work with regular breaks help reduce mental fatigue, improve concentration, and make tasks feel more manageable.

⏱ Pomodoro Cycle Summary

Cycle	Work Time	Break Time
1	25 min	5 min
2	25 min	5 min
3	25 min	5 min
4	25 min	15–30 min

🧠 Why It Works

- **Boosts focus** by creating time pressure
- **Prevents burnout** with regular breaks
- **Improves motivation** through visible progress
- **Reduces anxiety** by giving structure to your day

Within a few weeks, I noticed a big difference. I met my deadlines more consistently, and my stress levels went down. More importantly, I felt confident managing my work assignments. That experience taught me that time management isn't just about working harder — it's about working smarter and more intentionally.

Overcoming the Energy Barrier with unlocking the Power of a Healthy Body

"To keep the body in good health is a duty...otherwise we shall not be able to keep our mind strong and clear."—
Buddha

We live in a world that celebrates hustle, speed, and constant productivity. Yet no matter how ambitious your goals, how hard you work, or how big your dreams, none of it matters if your body isn't strong enough to sustain the journey. Your body is your vehicle. It carries you through life. Every step you take, every dream you chase, every relationship you build; it all depends on how well your body is functioning.

Let's dive into the details of what it means to eat whole, minimally processed foods, and why it's one of the most powerful habits for maintaining good health.

Whole foods are foods that are as close as possible to their natural state. They haven't been altered much, if at all, by industrial processing. They retain most of their original nutrients, fiber, and structure.

Minimally processed foods may be slightly altered for convenience or preservation, but they still look like what they came from and don't have added sugars, unhealthy fats, or artificial ingredients.

- Examples: Vegetable - Whole Foods -Fresh spinach, broccoli, carrots.

- Minimally Processed Alternatives - Prewashed salad greens, frozen veggies

Healthy eating habits may help you live longer and maintain an active lifestyle by keeping your body strong and resilient. When you consume adequate vitamins, minerals, and protein, it supports bone health and muscle function, reducing the risk of osteoporosis and frailty as you age.

Nutrient-dense foods help your immune system fend off illnesses and recover more quickly when you do get sick. Healthy foods, especially those high in antioxidants and omega-3 fatty acids, can enhance brain function, improve mood, and support emotional well-being. Eating a balanced diet helps regulate hunger hormones, increases satiety, and makes it easier to maintain a healthy weight.

High-fiber foods like fruits, vegetables, and whole grains promote good digestion and prevent constipation. It is great if you can include a mix of fruits, vegetables, whole grains, lean proteins, and healthy fats in your meals for balanced nutrition. Reducing your intake of processed foods, salty, sugary snacks, and saturated fats can lower your risk of chronic diseases.

For us to stay healthy, it's better to opt for fresh produce and whole foods whenever possible to maximize nutrient intake and minimize additives. Healthy eating is a long-term commitment, and making small, sustainable changes can have a significant impact over time.

When life gets busy, it's easy to put off routine checkups with your doctor. However, making sure you get your annual visits is one of the most important steps you can take to protect your health both now and in the future.[3]

One summer, I left the city and traveled to a place I had never been before — Bamberg, South Carolina, to visit my grandmother, Grandma Mary.

Life in the city was fast. I ate whatever was quick: fast food, chips, sugary drinks. My days were filled with noise and movement but not much nourishment. Still, I was excited to visit the state. I had no idea what was coming.

---

[3] Teladoc Health. 2024. "Whole Foods vs. Processed Foods." Harvard Health

That first morning, before the sun had fully risen, I was jolted awake by a loud alarm clock. Grandma Mary called out, "Time to go pick beans!"

I was still half asleep, but she was already dressed, walking outside, tying her hair back, and putting on her straw hat. Its brim wobbles with every step, flapping like a pancake in a breeze. I pulled myself together and followed her out to the fields. The air was fresh, the rows of plants seemed to go on forever, and the silence of the state felt peaceful… but my body was already tired.

After just 30 minutes in the field, bent over, moving under the hot sun. I felt exhausted. My head was light, my stomach churned, and my energy dropped fast. Meanwhile, Grandma Mary, over 70 years old, moved gracefully down the rows, bucket in hand, strong and steady.

"Grandma," I finally said, "how are you not tired?"

She smiled, wiped the sweat from her forehead, and said, "I take care of this body every day, baby. It gives me what I give it."

That hit me hard.

That afternoon, we sat down for a homemade meal with fresh beans, cornbread, tomatoes from the garden, and water with lemon—no fast food, no soda—just real food made with love.

And that's when it clicked.

Healthy food isn't a strict diet. It's fuel. It's nourishment. You don't have to eat perfectly to be healthy, just mindfully and moderately. Too much sugar, salt, or processed food puts out your fire. But balanced meals, real ingredients, and consistency? They help you thrive.

Overcoming Mental Health Barrier

When it comes to mental health obstacles, it's essential to approach them with a different mindset. This involves recognizing the importance of self-care, seeking support from professionals, and practicing self-compassion. As Therapy Changes suggests, "Turn apathy into action" by taking small steps towards recovery. You can "turn apathy into action" by starting small—taking manageable steps that gradually build momentum toward recovery. Even the smallest action, like setting a routine, reaching out for support, or practicing a healthy habit, can create a ripple effect that moves you forward.

Dealing With Distraction

It's costing us our focus, our energy, and our potential. Everywhere we turn, something competes for our attention—notifications, ads, endless scrolling, urgent messages, and the constant pressure to stay updated, liked, and followed.

We live in a world where attention is currency. Big businesses profit when we're distracted.
But we lose — our time, our clarity, and sometimes, our dreams.

Finding Purpose in a Time of Distraction and Loss

There are moments in life that shift everything — and for me, that moment was when COVID-19 shook the planet. I had planned to take the SHRM certification exam that year. I had studied, outlined a timeline, and felt ready to take that next step in my career. But suddenly, the world hit pause — and so did I.

When COVID-19 hit, life became capricious, unstable, and unpredictable, shifting without warning; my job changed overnight. I wasn't just handling normal HR issues anymore. I was responsible for ensuring compliance with COVID-19 protocols. This involved implementing new protocols, managing employee health reports, tracking vaccinations, and ensuring that weekly testing was conducted consistently and accurately.

People were scared. The rules kept changing. And I was one of the people who expected to figure it all out.

Responsibility Took Over My Life

There were late nights at the office, countless phone calls, and emergency meetings. I barely had time to sleep, let alone study. Every time I opened my SHRM prep book, I'd get an email about a new CDC update or a COVID-positive employee.

And then came the hardest part: my Uncle Sam passed away from COVID. A man who had been steady and strong in our family — gone.

Grief hit like a wave, and the news didn't help. Every headline felt like a punch. Death counts, shutdowns, protests, fear. It was impossible to stay focused. My mind was constantly racing, my heart heavy, and my spirit worn out.

Here's the truth: Distraction doesn't just make you slower, it makes you forget what you were aiming for in the first place. You start the day with goals. But before you know it, you've checked your phone 30 times, opened 10 apps, and your momentum is gone.

You can't build a business while chasing every trending topic. You can't improve your health while being pulled into dopamine loops every hour. You can't grow as a person if your mind is never still enough to hear your own thoughts.

Focus is the new superpower. In a distracted economy, the person who can stay focused for even an hour has a huge advantage.

The Power of the Right Environment

Success isn't just about talent or motivation. It's about where you place yourself when it's time to do the work.

Take Noah Lyles, one of the fastest sprinters in the world. Lyles also won an Olympic bronze in the 200 meters. He doesn't train just anywhere. He attends the National Training Center in Clermont, Florida, a facility designed for high performance. There are no distractions. No noise. Just elite athletes, world-class coaches, and laser focus. That environment helps him push past limits. It's *built* for greatness.

Now switch lanes. Picture J.K. Rowling, a British author, scribbling away in a coffee shop in Edinburgh. She wasn't in a fancy office or secluded mansion. She chose a warm, quiet place where her creativity could breathe — likely with her phone on Do Not Disturb. She wrote the first chapters of *Harry Potter* there, one cup of coffee at a time.

Different people. Different goals. Same principle: protect your focus by choosing the right environment.

Here's the truth: If you want to go deep to write, train, build, or think. You need to step away from the noise. You need to go where the distractions can't follow. That might be:

- A quiet library or workspace
- Your car is parked in peace.
- A gym where no one knows your name
- A corner of your house with your phone in another room

Focus isn't just willpower — it's setup.

You don't have to fight distractions all day. You have to design your space so distractions don't stand a chance.

Champions like Lyles train in silence. Writers like Rowling escape into their own worlds.
And when you want to create something meaningful, you should, too.

Chapter 7: STRATEGIES AND SUPPORT FOR UNSTOPPABLE GROWTH

Success is rarely achieved in isolation. Behind every great achievement lies a web of support. Mentors who guide, communities that uplift, and peers who walk the path alongside us. Whether you're pursuing academic, personal, or professional goals, surrounding yourself with the right people can make the journey not only easier but also more meaningful and sustainable.

Mentors are experienced individuals who offer wisdom, perspective, and guidance. They've often walked a similar path and can help navigate confrontations by offering insights you might not see on your own. A good mentor doesn't just give advice, but they challenge you, encourage your growth, and help you stay focused on long-term goals.

In every field, from business to the arts, stories abound of individuals whose success was sparked or sustained by the presence of a mentor. Steve Jobs mentored Mark Zuckerberg. Maya Angelou mentored Oprah Winfrey. These relationships often shape careers, character, and confidence.

A strong community provides more than just emotional support. It's a source of motivation, accountability, and shared knowledge. Whether it's a study group, a professional network, or an online forum, communities help normalize struggle and celebrate progress. When you see others overcoming obstacles similar to yours, it reinforces your own resilience.

Communities also foster collaboration, and they open doors to opportunities, resources, and diverse perspectives that can sharpen your thinking and broaden your possibilities. Simply put, we rise faster when we lift each other.

When you surround yourself with like-minded individuals - people who share your goals, values, or ambitions- you can provide constant motivation. These peers may not have all the answers, but they do offer camaraderie and a sense of shared purpose. Together, you can exchange ideas, hold each other accountable, and keep momentum alive, especially when the path feels lonely.

These relationships can evolve into partnerships, friendships, or even lifelong networks that continue to enrich your life long after the initial goal is achieved. In many cases, these connections outlast the success they help to achieve.

Building a support network is earned, not given; it requires intention and effort. Start by seeking out people who inspire you and align with your goals. Attend events, join groups, or reach out to those whose journeys resonate with you. Be genuine, show appreciation, and, importantly, be willing to give support in return.

It's also essential to maintain these relationships over time. Regular check-ins, honest conversations, and mutual encouragement keep the connection alive and meaningful.

Support Networks: How Finding the Right Help Launched My Career

There was a point in my life when I knew I was ready for more, not just a better salary, but a more meaningful, impactful career. I wanted a role that reflected my passion and potential. But I also knew I couldn't get there alone.

So, I took a simple first step: I went on LinkedIn and typed in career coach. That search led me to someone who felt like the perfect match. We began working together, diving deep into what I truly wanted in a career. Through our sessions, it became clear — my passion had always been in Human Resources. I loved supporting people, building teams, and helping organizations grow through their people.

My coach guided me not only in clarifying that vision, but also in creating a strategy to pursue it, refining my resume, strengthening my presence, and identifying the right kind of organizations where I could thrive. Along the way, I also had the unwavering support of my husband, Ed. His encouragement reminded me that I wasn't alone — that he believed in my abilities, even in the moments I doubted myself.

With the proper guidance, passing the SHRM test, and support behind me, I applied for a role that once felt out of reach: Vice President of Human Resources at a nonprofit organization. And I got it.

That experience taught me the power of seeking help, asking questions, and leaning into your support system, whether it's a professional coach, a digital network like LinkedIn, or the loved ones who cheer you on at home. Sometimes, the key to unlocking your next chapter is knowing you don't have to do it all alone.

Behind Every Success is a Team: The Truth About Getting Ahead

We often celebrate individual success stories—CEOs, athletes, artists, and entrepreneurs who seem to rise above the rest. But scratch beneath the surface, and a universal truth emerges: no one truly succeeds alone. Whether it's visible or not, every significant achievement is built on the foundation of teamwork, support, and collaboration.

Serena Williams is an American professional tennis player who has a dedicated coaching team. Every bestselling author has editors, proofreaders, and publicists. The truth? An invisible ensemble almost always supports solo acts.

Great ideas rarely come from echo chambers, and a strong team brings varied experiences, which sparks creativity and problem-solving. When you delegate tasks, it allows individuals to focus on their strengths while others cover complementary areas. Success is stressful. High expectations, tight deadlines, big decisions, and the fear of potential failure can weigh heavily, even when things are going well. That's why strong teams matter more than ever. A great team does more than share the workload. Teams provide encouragement, accountability, and resilience during tough times.

You will need constructive feedback from a trusted team that helps refine ideas and improve performance. When we're too close to our own ideas or performance, it's easy to overlook blind spots or opportunities for improvement. That's where honest, thoughtful input from others becomes invaluable.

A supportive team doesn't just echo our opinions; they challenge us, ask the right questions, and help us refine our thinking. Whether it's improving a project, reworking a pitch, or navigating a tough decision, their perspectives can sharpen our ideas and elevate the final result.

Feedback, when given with trust and received with openness, is not criticism. It's a collaboration. It transforms good work into great work and individual effort into collective success.

The most successful leaders invest in others. They understand that empowering teammates isn't just a generous act. It's strategic. When a team thrives, its members do too.

How to Build a Successful Team—and Make it Thrive.

Success isn't just about individual talent; it's about how well people work together toward a common goal. Whether you're leading a team or contributing to one, your ability to build and thrive within a team is a decisive factor in long-term achievement. First, start with a clear purpose. Every successful team begins with a shared vision. Without a clear goal, even talented individuals can work at cross-purposes. Why are we doing this? Ensure every team member understands not just what they're working on, but why it matters.

For example, I ask myself, "Why am I writing this book?" It's in my DNA, at my core, my personality as both a helper and an achiever. My greatest passion lies in empowering others to unlock their potential, particularly in building healthy and financial wealth and achieving a life of abundance.

Over the years, I have experienced firsthand the transformative power of cultivating wealth, prioritizing health, and embracing financial freedom. These experiences have not only changed my life but have also inspired me to share what I've learned with others.

Everyone deserves the opportunity to live life to the fullest, not just surviving, but truly thriving. Too often, people feel stuck, overwhelmed by financial stress, or unsure how to take the next step toward a healthier, more prosperous future. I want to change that narrative to success.

A strong team is not made of clones. It's built on diverse skills, perspectives, and experiences.

Everyone has strengths and weaknesses. Start by identifying each team member's strengths.
Then delegate tasks based on ability and passion. It's imperative to respect different working styles and communication preferences.

A great team communicates openly and often. Effective communication is the foundation of every high-performing team. As companies scale, one of the most common and usually underestimated challenges they face is a breakdown in communication. What works in a small team of 5-10 people quickly starts to unravel when there are dozens, hundreds, or thousands of employees across departments, locations, and time zones. It is good to use regular check-ins, clear messaging, and active listening. I like structure, so I maintain it daily. Encourage feedback, both giving and receiving, without ego.

A successful team needs to create a culture of trust. When you say you are going to work on projects, keep your commitments, and support others in theirs. In your daily meeting, inform the others about the project's status. If there are any delays or you encounter issues, please contact the other team members. Everyone on the team should feel comfortable sharing ideas or making mistakes, and avoid blaming themselves; instead, they should focus on finding solutions.

Success brings pressure, and no one thrives in isolation. The best teams strike a balance between support and structure. Here's how to cultivate a culture where people feel empowered, not just evaluated.

Leaders don't wait for the finish line to give recognition; they acknowledge small wins, consistent effort, and creative problem-solving along the way. Progress fuels motivation.

Great leaders and teammates ask, "How are you holding up?" not just "Is it done yet?"
Create space for honest conversations and emotional well-being. Remember that high morale sustains high performance. Accountability works best when it's rooted in respect, not pressure.
Offer feedback constructively, set clear expectations, and lead with empathy. We grow together, not through fear but through trust.

Great teams don't just perform, they grow. And growth comes from the ability to adapt.

Roles, responsibilities, processes, and even goals may need to shift as the team evolves. Flexibility is a strength, not a weakness. Leaders don't just reward people for checking boxes but create space for fresh ideas, creative thinking, and experimentation.

When a team embraces feedback and change with curiosity and courage, it stays strong, agile, and ready for whatever comes next.

Whether you're in a formal leadership role or not, your behavior sets the tone for the entire team.

Show up prepared, positive, and proactive. Your attitude and effort influence the energy of those around you. All team members model collaboration, humility, and resilience. Be the person who lifts others, listens before speaking, and bounces back from setbacks with grace.

Be the kind of teammate you'd want to work with. Set the standard through your actions, not just your words. Strong teams aren't built overnight — they're shaped every day by how each person shows up. Leadership isn't a title; it's a choice.

Building and thriving in a successful team isn't about perfection; it's about progress, connection, and shared commitment. When individuals align around a purpose, support each other, and hold one another to high standards, they don't just achieve goals. They grow together.

Because in the end, teams don't just produce great results. They create great experiences.

The Turnaround: How Empathy and Intelligence Built a High-Performing Team

A few years ago, a mid-sized marketing agency was struggling. Profits were flat, employee turnover was high, and morale was worse. The founder, Angela, was brilliant—sharp, numbers-driven, and laser-focused on results. But her leadership style? Let's just say… she led with strategy, not with soul.

That changed the day one of her most talented team members quit—abruptly. On their way out, they said, "You care more about KPIs (Key Performance Indicators) than people. I can't grow in a place where I feel invisible."

That stuck with Angela. She didn't double down. She paused. And then she changed course.

Angela began researching emotional intelligence and leadership psychology. She brought in a coach, not to boost sales—but to help her listen better, communicate clearly, and connect more deeply.

And then, she did something powerful: She gathered her team and said, "I've been leading with my head and not enough with my heart. That changes now." She started:

- Holding one-on-one check-ins—not just about projects, but about people.

- Celebrating progress and effort, not just results.
- Creating space for ideas from every level, not just the top.

Team members began opening up. Trust grew. Turnover dropped. And with psychological safety in place, innovation took off.

Within a year, not only had they increased revenue by 30%, but they also became one of the top-rated places to work in their city. Angela realized something that changed her leadership forever:

Business intelligence tells you what to do. Emotional intelligence tells you how to lead while doing it. And empathy? That's what makes people stay. The agency didn't grow just because it had smart strategies. They grew because they built a culture where smart, cared-for people could thrive.

Chapter 8: FOUNDATION OF SUCCESS

Many successful leaders stress that financial literacy and disciplined budgeting are the backbone of true achievement—because without them, earning a high income alone does not guarantee long-term success; without careful planning, money can quickly disappear through impulsive spending, debt, or missed opportunities for investment.

Saving money when you don't have a lot can feel overwhelming, but even small changes can create powerful momentum. The key is to maximize what you have and build smart habits that grow over time.

Here are practical, realistic ways to save money when funds are tight:

1. Track Every Dollar

Knowing where your money is going is the first—and most powerful—step in taking control of your finances. Whether you use a pencil and notebook, a spreadsheet, or a free Apps like *Mint* or *EveryDollar* help you track your spending, allowing you to see the full picture. You can't change what you don't measure.

Why is budgeting so important? Because it gives you a clear and honest view of your finances.

A good budget shows you:

- How much money is coming in
- How much is going out
- How fast is money moving
- Where your money is being spent
- And most importantly, whether you earn enough to cover your expenses

Starting a budget can feel uncomfortable. It might reveal that your current lifestyle is unsustainable—and that's never easy to face. Additionally, budgeting requires time and effort, especially in the initial stages.

But here's the truth: if you want to make real, positive changes, you need to know where you stand financially. When you take control of your money, you'll feel more empowered, less stressed, and more confident in your decisions. A budget provides clarity, calm, and control.

A Common Budgeting Scenario

Have you ever had a little money saved, only to be surprised by an annual bill—like car taxes or a warehouse membership—just when you thought you were getting ahead? Because these bills only come once a year, it's easy to forget about them. When they hit, you might end up:

- Draining your bank account
- Charging it to a credit card
- Or stressing because the money just isn't there

It's a horrible feeling. But here's the good news: with just a little planning, you can avoid this.

2. Planning Makes All the Difference

Imagine setting aside a small amount from each paycheck, and when that once-a-year bill comes, you already have the money saved. No stress. No surprises. Just relief. Now imagine that kind of planning for every bill—daily, weekly, monthly, quarterly, or annual. That peace of mind is what budgeting brings. It takes practice and discipline, but you can do it.

Let's get started by building your very first budget.

What You Need to Begin

Before creating your budget, make sure you have the following:

- Checking account: This will be your active account for daily spending and short-term savings.

- At least one savings account: This is for long-term savings or goals like buying a car, house, etc.

Even if you only have one physical checking account, your budget will break it down into virtual categories—think of it like using digital "envelopes" for different spending purposes.

Using a Spreadsheet or Notebook

It's highly recommended that you use a spreadsheet tool like Microsoft Excel or Google Sheets. It's easier to manage and can be automated if you're comfortable with basic functions or macros. If you're not tech-savvy, a good notebook and calculator will work just fine. The key is to stay consistent. Your budget will include three main sections:

1. **Planning Sheet**

    - List all your income, bills, and savings goals
    - Organized by frequency (monthly, annual, etc.)

2. **Budget Sheet**

    - Gives a real-time view of your checking account
    - Shows what your money is currently allocated for

3. **Credit Card Sheet**

    - Tracks which bills are paid by which credit card

    - Helps when you get a new card or need to update payment info. **(For a detailed breakdown of budgeting steps, refer to Appendix A.)**

Let's Talk About High-Expense Credit Card Debt

According to the Federal Reserve. (2025). While credit card ownership has increased over the past decade, carrying a credit card balance has become less prevalent. In 2024, 46 percent of credit card owners said they carried a balance at least once during the prior 12 months. Adults with income under $100,000 were more likely to carry credit card balances from month to month.

My friend, Marie, was always good at making things look effortless. The high-cost outfits, the brunches, the last-minute weekend trips, the gifts she bought for others, "just because." On the outside, she seemed like someone who had it all together—young, successful, and living her best life.

But behind the scenes, Marie was quietly drowning.

It started with one credit card. Then another. Then, a store card that promised "special savings" on her first purchase. At first, it felt manageable. Her minimum payments were low, and she figured, *"I'll pay it off next month."* But next month turned into next year.

When her rent increased, she leaned on her cards a little more. When her car broke down, she didn't have an emergency fund, so she charged the $900 repair. By the time her best friend's wedding came around, she had no cash left, so she put the dress, the flight, and the hotel on her card, convincing herself it was just a once-in-a-lifetime event.

Her balance crossed $10,000 before she realized she had a problem. The monthly interest alone was over $200, and most of her payments were only going toward that interest, not the actual debt. Each swipe now came with a knot in her stomach. She wasn't buying joy anymore. She was buying time. Borrowed time.

The truth hit her hard one afternoon while trying to buy groceries. Her card was declined. Twice. She stood in the checkout line with people behind her, panic rising in her chest. She had a full cart and no money to pay for it. Embarrassed and overwhelmed, she left the store with tears in her eyes and an empty fridge at home.

That moment became her wake-up call.

Marie went home and laid every credit card statement on the table. She added up the balances, the interest rates, and the minimum payments. For the first time, she faced the numbers. It was brutal. But it was honest. And from that moment, she made a decision: *No more pretending. No more living a life I can't afford. No more debt controlling me.*

She called her credit card companies, negotiated lower interest rates where possible, and began building a real budget—one that didn't rely on plastic. She stopped using her cards completely and found remote part-time work on weekends to increase her income. Every extra dollar went toward paying off her highest-interest card first.

It wasn't glamorous. There were no brunches, no new clothes, no trips. But there was peace. Slowly, Marie saw the balances go down. And for the first time in years, she slept soundly, knowing she was in control again.

It took her two years to pay it all off. The day she made her final credit card payment, she didn't go out to celebrate. She sat in her apartment, looked around, and whispered to herself, *"Freedom."*

The Lesson: Credit card debt doesn't just steal your money—it steals your peace, your sleep, and your future. It's easy to fall in and hard to climb out, but it is possible. Marie's story isn't unique. It's real. It's common. And it's fixable.

The first step? Face the numbers. The next step? Take control. And never again give a piece of your future away for something you don't really need today.

- If your card has a high interest rate (APR), even small balances can grow quickly. Carrying a $1,000 balance at 23% - 25% APR means you'll pay hundreds in interest if you don't pay it off quickly.

- If you charge $1,000 on a credit card with a 23% APR, here's what that means: Over the span of one year (12 months), you'd owe $230 in interest—this is simply $0.23 \times \$1,000 = \$230$.

- High balances relative to your limit hurt your credit utilization ratio, which can lower your credit score. Even if you make payments on time, having a large outstanding balance can work against you.

The more you owe, the more pressure you feel. High minimum payments can eat into your monthly budget and make it hard to save or cover other bills. Living under that weight can be exhausting.

Chapter 9: DEVELOP THE HABITS OF SUCCESSFUL PEOPLE

Successful people often own the first hour of their day. Whether it's journaling, exercising, meditating, or reading, what matters is starting the day *intentionally*, not reactively.

"Win the morning, win the day."

They set clear, purposeful goals. They know what they're working toward and *why*. Goals aren't vague wishes; they're broken down into focused, trackable actions. I use SMART goals (Specific, Measurable, Achievable, Relevant, Time-bound) and revisit and revise them regularly. A **SMART goal** is a structured way of setting goals to make them clear, realistic, and achievable. The acronym **SMART** stands for:

1. **Specific** – The goal is clear and well-defined.
   Example: "I want to improve my fitness." → "I want to run 3 miles without stopping."

2. **Measurable** – You can track progress and know when it's achieved.
   Example: "I want to lose 10 pounds" instead of "I want to lose weight."

3. **Achievable** – The goal is realistic given your resources and constraints.

   Example: Aiming to save $200 per month if your budget allows, rather than $2,000.

4. **Relevant** – The goal aligns with your broader objectives and values.

   Example: Saving money for a home down payment instead of something unrelated if buying a home is your priority.

5. **Time-bound** – The goal has a clear deadline or timeframe.

   Example: "I will complete an online certification course in 3 months.

Devaughn was a talented barber in a town. Everyone knew him for his skills, his stories, and that unbeatable fade he gave every Friday. Business was steady, but Devaughn always felt something was missing. He was working hard, staying busy, but not really moving forward.

One night, after a long day, he sat in his empty shop and asked himself: "What am I really working toward?"

That question changed everything.

He pulled out a notebook and wrote: "I want to own three barbershops in five years and teach young people how to build careers in this industry."

Boom. That was his purpose.

From that day on, Devaughn worked with *direction*. He created a business plan. Took courses in leadership and finance. Started saving with intention. And every week, he tracked his progress not just his income, but how many steps he was taking toward that bigger vision.

He hired his first apprentice. A year later, opened shop number two.
By year five? Three thriving shops and a training program that helped young men in his community turn clippers into careers.

When people asked how he did it, he said: "The hustle was always there—I just finally gave it a destination."

Successful People Invest in Continuous Learning

"Your income rarely exceeds your personal development." – Jim Rohn

Successful people consistently invest in continuous learning, leveraging books, podcasts, courses, and mentors to stay ahead and adapt in a rapidly changing world. This commitment is not just a cliché. it's a proven strategy among top performers in business, leadership, and entrepreneurship.

Lifelong learning is a mindset that fosters curiosity, adaptability, and resilience —critical traits for sustained success.

Books remain a foundational tool for deep learning and reflection. Successful leaders often recommend classics such as *"The 7 Habits of Highly Effective People" by Stephen Covey or "Good to Great"* by Jim Collins.

Not everyone starts with the same advantages, but one thing is clear: *education is a door-opener.* My husband and I have interviewed hundreds of successful people—entrepreneurs, artists, tech developers, CEOs, and community leaders. Many of them came from broken homes, poverty, or challenging school experiences. A few dropped out of high school — including me. Yes, me

But do you know the one thing we all had in common before we reached our goals? We went back to school to earn our high school diploma or GED.

It is one of the most important steps you can take to build a successful and stable future. It's more than just getting a diploma—it's about opening doors, gaining confidence, and setting the foundation for everything that comes next.

It increases your earning power. A high school diploma is the minimum requirement for most jobs. On average, high school graduates earn significantly more than those who drop out.

College can be a powerful launchpad for success, especially in fields like medicine, law, and academia, where advanced education is essential. But I also recognize that college is not the right path for everyone—and that's perfectly okay. Success does not come in one shape or through one path. Look at Steve Jobs and Mark Zuckerberg, American computer programmer and entrepreneur, best known as the co-founder and CEO of Meta Platforms (formerly Facebook). They dropped out of college, but they never stopped learning. They read, explored, asked questions, took risks, and pushed themself to grow in every way possible. That's the key: *You still have to grow.* Whether it's through a trade, college, starting a business, self-education, mentorship, or hands-on experience, your growth can't stop just because you did not go the traditional route. The world belongs to people who stay curious, keep learning, and never settle.

Reading widely across disciplines and industries broadens perspective and sparks innovative thinking. It improves focus, concentration, and strengthens neural connections, while also building new ones and enhancing memory and cognitive function.

The more you read, the more you know about history, culture, science, and human behavior. Knowledge builds confidence and competence in conversation and decision-making.

It expands vocabulary and communication skills. You will be able to speak, write, listen, and comprehend. Reading builds empathy and perspective. Reading fiction, memoirs, and diverse viewpoints helps you: Cultivate empathy and emotional intelligence.

Can you believe that reading reduces stress (especially fiction)? It can be meditative. It offers an escape from daily pressures, lowers stress levels, and promotes relaxation.

Some people may not enjoy reading, but podcasts can offer many of the same benefits in a more engaging and flexible format. Here's how podcasts help, especially for those who are not into reading:

Learning in Motion: Podcasts and Targeted Courses

In today's fast-paced world, staying sharp means staying curious—and few tools make that easier than podcasts. With just a tap, you can access fresh, up-to-date insights from thought leaders, innovators, and industry experts. Shows like *Power Skills for Success* delve into essential topics such as curiosity, communication, and lifelong learning—traits that directly shape how we grow, lead, and succeed.

One of the biggest advantages of podcasts is their flexibility. For busy professionals, they offer a way to learn on the go—during a commute, while exercising, cooking, or even walking the dog. Unlike reading, podcasts don't require your full visual attention, making them easier to integrate into daily life. For auditory learners or those with learning differences, such as dyslexia or ADHD, the spoken format can be more engaging and accessible. The tone, energy, and personality of each speaker add a human touch that turns information into a conversation.

Beyond convenience, podcasts deliver real value: new ideas, motivation, practical knowledge, and fresh perspectives from around the world. They help improve listening skills, expose listeners to different voices and vocabulary, and can even boost confidence when applying new insights to everyday life.

Alongside informal learning through podcasts, more structured education—like targeted online courses, workshops, or leadership development programs—can take your skills to the next level. When chosen intentionally, these experiences offer a high return on investment. Whether it's an MBA, a certification course, or a short workshop, focused learning environments help deepen expertise, sharpen leadership skills, and create momentum toward personal and professional growth.

In short, advancement doesn't always require a classroom or a textbook. Sometimes, all it takes is pressing play—or choosing the right course at the right time.

How Podcasts Became My Best Friend While Learning Spanish

When I began learning Spanish, I struggled to maintain a daily habit. I didn't have time to sit down with a textbook, and I often felt stuck.

Then I found Spanish podcasts and everything changed. Suddenly, I was learning on the go:

- On my drive to work

- While doing tasks at my job

- During workouts at the gym

I wasn't just studying Spanish. I was living in it. The voices, the conversations, the stories — they became part of my routine. After a while, I wasn't just listening — I was thinking in Spanish. I was even dreaming in Spanish.

Podcasts turned passive time into learning time. They made Spanish feel natural, not forced. They were my best friend in the learning journey, always there, always speaking Spanish to me.

And that's when I realized: fluency doesn't start in a classroom. Sometimes, it starts with your earbuds.

When I was learning Spanish, nothing helped more than going to Málaga. I found myself surrounded by a group of friends who spoke Spanish almost exclusively. We'd go out for tapas, sharing plates of *paella*, sipping glasses of *Rioja*, and soaking in the warm, golden evenings.

In the background, the music of Manu Chao would play — *Me Gustas Tú*, a song by a French artist of Spanish descent. It became the soundtrack of that summer.

Everything about that time — the food, the music, the laughter, the rhythm of the language around me — made the learning come alive. It wasn't just vocabulary or grammar anymore. Spanish became something I felt. The atmosphere was ineffable, beyond words. And because of that, the words are stuck.

Conversations make learning stick, and dialogues can be more memorable than text. Real voices telling real stories make concepts easier to relate to.

Mentorship is a powerful accelerator for personal and professional development. The right mentors provide not only advice but also open doors to new opportunities and networks. Modern approaches to mentorship emphasize collaboration and shared projects, aiming for "super mentors" who can make a transformative impact.

How to apply practical strategies?

Curate Your "Media Diet": Deliberately choose books, podcasts, and courses that align with your current goals and challenges.

Apply what you learn: The value of learning comes from applying it to seek opportunities to put new knowledge into practice.

Build a learning ecosystem: Combine self-study with community learning, resource sharing, and mentorship for a holistic approach.

Stay curious and open: Embrace a growth mindset, remain open to new ideas, and be willing to adapt as circumstances change.

Success isn't just what you do: it's how you connect. Top performers actively listen, ask questions, and speak with clarity and purpose. Emotional intelligence is a cornerstone of influence.

Successful people build strong relationships and a team where no one succeeds alone. Successful people intentionally build a network of mentors, collaborators, and supporters, and they give as much as they take.

Finding Myself in Stories: From the South Bronx to Something More

I was born in Harlem and later moved to the South Bronx. Growing up in poverty, I've always looked for stories of people who came from where I came from — people whose lives could reflect my own, and who could serve as role models.

One story that hit close to home was that of Justice Sonia Sotomayor. Like me, she grew up in the South Bronx. Her path wasn't easy, but what struck me most was how real and honest she was about her struggles — especially when she said she didn't know how to study as a young student. Instead of giving up, she asked the smartest person in the room for help. At first, that person thought it was a strange question, but they helped her — and that moment changed everything. She learned how to study, mastered it, and never looked back.

Today, she's an Associate Justice of the Supreme Court. I didn't follow the same path. I never wanted to be a lawyer — but in our own ways, we both found a way out of difficult circumstances. We both chose to thrive, and you should too—success is waiting.

The Power of Saying "No"

Too often, we acquiesce to the demands of others—not because we agree, but because we fear disappointing them. We say "yes" when we want to say "no," stretching ourselves thin to maintain peace or avoid guilt. But constantly acquiescing to please others comes at a cost: your time, your energy, your boundaries. Saying "no" isn't selfish—it's an act of self-respect. It's recognizing that your priorities matter, and your well-being isn't up for negotiation. The power of "no" is the power to choose *you*, without apology.

Saying "yes" to every request, meeting, or opportunity may seem like the path to success, but in reality, it often leads to burnout and distraction. Successful people understand that every "yes" is also a "no" to something else, often something more important.

Learning to say no is not about being dismissive or inflexible. It's about clarity, knowing your priorities, and aligning your time with what matters most. Whether it's declining a non-essential meeting or turning down a project that doesn't align with your goals, every no is an investment in your focus.

Equally important is the ability to delegate. Trying to do everything yourself is not a sign of strength. It's a barrier to flourishing. Successful leaders and professionals know that their time is best spent on tasks that match their unique strengths and responsibilities.

Delegation isn't about offloading work—it's about empowering others, building trust, and ensuring the right person is handling the right task. Whether you're a manager, entrepreneur, or part of a team, mastering delegation creates space for innovation, strategic thinking, and personal well-being.

Ultimately, protecting your time requires discipline. It's not always easy to say no. It's not always comfortable to let go of control. But those who do it well are the ones who rise above the noise and make consistent, meaningful progress toward their goals.

The truth is, success doesn't come from doing more; it comes from doing *what matters*. Say no to the rest. Delegate the rest. And protect your time like the valuable asset it is.

The Power of One Hour

People often tell me, *"You're always so busy."* And they're not wrong. Life is full—work, family, responsibilities, unexpected detours. But a while ago, I realized something important: being busy wasn't an excuse to put my dreams on hold.

So, I made a decision. I started waking up just one hour earlier each day. One quiet, uninterrupted hour not for emails, not for others, but for *me*. That hour became sacred. I used it to write, plan, learn, and build what I wanted for my future.

It wasn't always easy. Some mornings I was tired. Some days, I didn't see immediate results. But I kept showing up for myself.

We all get 24 hours in a day. That's the one thing we all have in common. There will always be delays, distractions, and detours—but there should be no excuses. If something truly matters to you, you find a way, even if it's just one hour at a time.

That small habit changed everything for me. And it can be for you, too.

Chapter 10: BREAKING BARRIERS IN SPECIFIC AREAS

We often talk about breaking barriers as if it's a one-time, life-changing moment. However, the truth is that most breakthroughs occur quietly in very specific areas of our lives. It's not always about changing the whole world overnight. Sometimes, it's about pushing past one boundary at a time.

Maybe it's the fear of speaking up in meetings. Hesitation to ask for help. The belief that you're not "technical" enough, "experienced" enough, or "ready" enough. These aren't global limitations—they're personal ones. And they can be just as powerful.

Breaking barriers doesn't always mean going big. It means getting intentional.

Ask yourself: *What's one specific area where I'm holding back?* Is it your health/weight? Your relationship? Your creativity? Your confidence at work? Your education? Your finance?

Start there.

Challenge the story you've been telling yourself. Replace *"I can't"* with *"What if I tried?"* Take one small action that disrupts the old patterns. Progress often begins with something as simple as showing up differently.

When you focus on breaking barriers in specific areas, something powerful happens: momentum builds. Confidence grows. You begin to see that change is possible and not just in theory, but in your everyday reality.

You don't have to transform everything at once. You just have to start somewhere specific.

Whether you're climbing the corporate ladder or building a business from the ground up, career advancement is about more than just working hard; it's about working smart and strategically. Success doesn't happen by accident; it's the result of focused actions, continuous learning, and intentional growth.

Here are key strategies to help you excel, no matter what your path:

Master Your Craft: You Have to Become a Junkie

If you want to rise above the noise—whether in business, sports, the arts, acting, producing, writing, entrepreneurship, or leadership—you can't just be interested in what you do. You have to be obsessed. Talent alone is never enough. Inspiration fades. Passion cools. But mastery? Mastery sticks. And it only comes to those who are addicted—not to fame, applause, or outcomes—but to the process itself.

Yes, you have to become a junkie. Not in the destructive sense. Not the kind of dependency that ruins lives—but the kind that builds legacies. The type of devotion that says, "I can't go a day without getting better."

This isn't a cute slogan. It's a reality shared by the highest performers across every field. The world's best don't dabble. They devour. They inhale their craft. They study it, stretch it, challenge it, and submit to it daily. They need it.

Denzel Washington: An Actor Obsessed

Denzel Washington is not just one of the greatest actors of our time—he's a man obsessed with excellence. Early in his career, he didn't just show up for roles—he broke down scripts word by word, studied the psychology of his characters, and rehearsed relentlessly. He was known for asking directors detailed questions about motivation, scene intention, and backstory—because he wasn't satisfied with being good. He wanted to be unforgettable.

Even after multiple Oscars and decades of fame, Denzel didn't let up. When preparing for Fences, a role that required intense emotional labor and depth, he spent months rehearsing the stage version before filming the movie. Why? Because he wasn't addicted to awards— he was obsessed with honing his craft.

Sara Blakely: Self-Taught Billionaire

Before she became the youngest self-made female billionaire, Sara Blakely spent two years developing the prototype for Spanx. She didn't know the fashion industry. She had no design background. However, she was deeply committed to solving problems for women. She cold-called manufacturers, wrote her own patent, and pitched her product door-to-door. She failed dozens of times. But she never stopped learning, testing, and improving.

She didn't wait for permission. She became addicted to figuring it out.

Be So Good They Beg for Your Service

I was getting my hair done recently, and something stood out. In the same salon, there was a stylist named Charlize. She wasn't just busy—she was booked solid—weeks in advance. Clients were literally begging her and were willing to pay above her normal rates just to get in her chair.

Why? Because Charlize was the best at what she does.

She didn't need to advertise or chase clients. Her work spoke for itself. Her reputation did the heavy lifting. People weren't just willing to pay—they were eager to. That kind of demand is built, not stumbled upon.

It stems from mastery, consistency, and consistently delivering excellence. Charlize became a name people trusted. And that kind of value is magnetic.

Now, here's the thing: that could be you.

No matter what your field, whether you're a coach, a consultant, an artist, a fashion designer, a YouTuber, a barber, a tech pro, or a business owner, you have the same opportunity. When you master your craft, respect your clients, and deliver results that exceed expectations, your work becomes your best marketing tool.

You don't need to be famous. You just need to be so good that they can't ignore you.

Why It Matters

Ambitious people think differently. They don't settle. They push boundaries. Being around them challenges you to level up. Their energy is contagious, their mindset is expansive, and their habits are aligned with progress.

When you're surrounded by people who are driven, focused, and forward-thinking, you naturally start to adopt similar behaviors. Conversations shift from complaining to creating, from doubting to doing.

Tailored advice for professionals seeking extraordinary outcomes in competitive fields.

Sales and Business Growth: Strategies for Achieving Extraordinary Outcomes in Competitive Fields

In competitive industries, average efforts lead to average results. If you're serious about standing out, whether you're a sales professional, entrepreneur, business leader, entertainment artist, or hair stylist, you need strategies that go beyond the basics. Advancement didn't happen by chance. It's intentional, strategic, and driven by action.

Here are key principles to drive extraordinary outcomes in sales and business:

1. **Know Your Market Inside and Out**

   Deep understanding creates deep trust. Study your target market's main points, desires, language, and decision-making patterns. The more intimately you understand your audience, the more effectively you can position your offer as the solution they've been waiting for.

2. **Build Relationships, Not Just Pipelines**

   People do business with people they trust. In the workplace, networking and collaboration can accelerate your visibility and credibility. As an entrepreneur, relationships are the foundation of referrals, funding, and growth. Never underestimate the power of connection.

   Stay connected to the right ambitious people.

   Success isn't just about what you know—it's also about who you surround yourself with. The people in your circle influence your mindset, your energy, your standards, and your vision. If you want to grow, achieve more, and stay motivated, one of the most powerful things you can do is stay connected to the right ambitious people.

Sales are about service. Business growth is about trust. People don't buy from pitches—they buy from people. Prioritize relationships over transactions. Deliver value early and often, and build a network based on credibility, authenticity, and long-term vision.

A while back, I needed some repairs done around the house. Like many people, I found a contractor through social media. I didn't know what to expect, but when he showed up, something unexpected happened.

We talked about the job for maybe 15 minutes. Then he started telling me about his mom, his dog, and a few stories about his life. It wasn't just small talk—it felt real. He wasn't just trying to close a deal; he was building a relationship.

After that first visit, we kept in touch. He would text me on my birthday, and even on Mother's Day, because he'd met my kids and remembered their names and how important family was to me. He wasn't just "the handyman" anymore. He became someone I trusted.

Here's the lesson:

In business and in life, people don't just remember the service—they remember the connection. When you take the time to truly get to know someone, to see them beyond the transaction, you build something money can't buy: loyalty.

Whether you're in sales, running a business, or just trying to grow your network—remember this:

People may hire you for a skill, but they stay because of the relationship.

It's not about being overly personal—it's about being human. Show people you care, and they'll never forget you.

3. **Focus on Solutions, Not Features**

Customers and clients care less about what your product is and more about what it does for them. Whether selling a service or scaling a business, always lead with the outcome. Show them how their life or business improves by working with you.

4. **Systemize What Works**

   Lasting success isn't sustainable without structure. Track your sales process, automate where possible, and create repeatable systems for onboarding, fulfillment, and follow-up. What gets measured gets managed—and what gets streamlined scales.

5. **Be Obsessively Customer-Centric**

   Businesses that thrive in competitive markets obsess over customer experience. Listen more than you speak. Overdeliver. Turn customers into raving fans who refer, review, and return. Word-of-mouth is still one of the most powerful growth tools.

6. **Stay Relentlessly Consistent**

   Consistency beats intensity. Show up every day. Follow up. Refine your pitch. Reach out again. The professionals who win are the ones who keep going, especially when others give up.

Military Advancement: Principles for Rising Through the Ranks with Purpose and Excellence

Advancing in any field requires more than time in service; it takes discipline, leadership, self-awareness, and a clear commitment to growth. In a structured and highly competitive environment, those who rise to the top are not just competent—they are consistent, mission-driven, and respected by their peers and superiors alike.

If you're seeking advancement in any field, here are key principles that will set you apart:

1. Master the Fundamentals

No one advances without first excelling at the basics. Know your responsibilities inside and out. Be the person who is reliable, detail-oriented, and prepared. Excellence in the fundamentals is the foundation for leadership.

2. Lead from Every Position

You don't need a title to lead. Whether you're a junior enlisted member or a non-commissioned officer, lead by example. Display integrity, professionalism, and initiative. Real leadership is noticed even when it's not officially assigned.

3. **Stay Fit—Physically and Mentally**

   Advancement requires you to be mission-ready in every way. Prioritize physical training, but don't neglect mental sharpness. Seek out educational opportunities, master technical skills, and stay current with doctrine and policy.

4. **Seek Mentorship and Give It Back**

   Learn from those who've walked the path before you. Ask questions, accept feedback, and apply what you learn. As you grow, invest in others coming up behind you—being a leader means lifting others as you climb.

5. **Take Every Evaluation Seriously**

   Every evaluation, test, and review matters. Approach them with complete preparation. Know what's expected for promotion and go above and beyond. Keep a record of your accomplishments and be prepared to communicate your value clearly.

6. **Embody the Core Values**

   Whether it's duty, honor, respect, or excellence—live out your branch's core values daily. Promotions may be based on performance, but true advancement is earned through character.

"Steel and Spirit: The Rise of Ann E. Dunwoody"

Ann E. Dunwoody grew up in a modest family in Fort Bragg, North Carolina, where hard work and integrity were valued above all else. Her father served in the military, and her mother instilled in her the importance of discipline and perseverance. But Ann wasn't content with simply following the expected path—she wanted her life to make a difference.

At 18, she pursued a career in the U.S. Army—not out of necessity, but purpose.

Day one: basic training. Grueling drills. Shouts that pushed her beyond her comfort zone. While many struggled under the physical and mental strain, Ann met every challenge with determination. She wasn't always the strongest or fastest, but she was consistent. She listened. She learned. She led.

Over the years, she rose through the ranks, not by chasing titles, but by pursuing excellence. As a leader, she never asked her soldiers to do something she wouldn't do herself. Her motto was simple: "Earn their trust before you ask for their respect."

Her teams followed her not out of obligation, but because Ann inspired confidence in themselves, in the mission, and in something bigger than any one individual.

In 2008, she became the first female four-star general in U.S. Army history, breaking barriers while demonstrating that leadership is rooted in service, integrity, and relentless effort.

Throughout her career, she emphasized the importance of purpose, excellence, and perseverance. She showed that true leadership isn't about rank or recognition—it's about lifting others and inspiring them to achieve more than they thought possible. "Her story shows what's possible—you can be this, too."

Chapter 11: CELEBRATING MILESTONES AND PROGRESS

In a world that often only celebrates big wins, it's easy to overlook the quiet victories: showing up on tough days, learning a new skill, finishing what you started. But these are the moments that shape character. By recognizing small achievements, we reinforce the truth that progress is not always loud. it's often steady, quiet, and deeply personal. And each acknowledgment, no matter how modest, fuels confidence, encourages perseverance, and reminds us that we are moving forward one step, one effort, one milestone at a time.

On Personal Growth:

Marking achievements, no matter how small, validates hard work and dedication, which is essential for building self-esteem and resilience.

It encourages reflection on the journey, not just the result, helping individuals appreciate incremental progress and stay committed to long-term goals.

In Organizations:

Recognizing milestones at work aligns teams with a shared vision, inspires individuals, and reinforces a culture of appreciation and achievement.

A junior employee finishes their first major project on time. Their manager brings it up in the team meeting and says, "Let's take a moment to recognize this win. It took focus and follow-through." The recognition boosts morale and sets a tone for valuing growth and development.

A student who struggled all semester earns a passing grade through hard work. The school counselor writes them a note:
"This progress shows what commitment looks like. You should be proud."
Acknowledging effort, not just outcome, builds long-term motivation.

How to Maintain Momentum After Initial Success

1. **Celebrate — But Don't Settle**

   Acknowledge the win, but treat it as a checkpoint, not the finish line.
   Tip: Say to yourself or your team, "This is proof we can do it—now let's build on it."

2. **Set the Next Goal Immediately**

   Success creates energy, but that energy fades without a new target.
   Tip: After achieving one milestone, ask: "What's the next level up?"

   Example: You passed basic training—what's next? MOS, aka Mastering your Military Occupational Specialty, aka MOS? Leading others? Earning a specialized qualification?

3. **Break Progress into Small, Visible Wins**

   Break larger goals into smaller tasks so you keep seeing results.
   Tip: Track your progress weekly. Visual progress boosts motivation.

"I improved my PT score by 5 points this week" keeps the fire burning more than a vague "Get in shape."

4. **Surround yourself with forward-thinking people**

   Surround yourself with those who push forward—even after wins.

   Tip: Join a peer group, team, or mentor circle where success is normal but complacency isn't.

5. **Revisit Your Why**

   Remember what drove you to start. Was it proving something to yourself? Supporting your family? Breaking a generational pattern?

   Tip: Write down your original motivation and read it when motivation dips.

6. **Turn Success into Service**

   Teach, mentor, or lift others. When you help someone else succeed, you automatically raise your own bar.

   Tip: Ask: "Who can benefit from what I've just learned?"

Sustaining Progress and Breaking New Ground

Success is not the end—it's the invitation to begin again, but better, sharper, and stronger. After the applause fades and the medals are hung, a deeper question emerges: How do you keep growing when the first mountain has been climbed?

True excellence isn't just found in rising—it's found in the discipline to sustain and the courage to expand.

Sustaining Growth: Discipline Over Hype

Initial victories feel powerful—but they can be deceptive. Momentum, if not maintained, becomes memory. Sustaining growth requires daily consistency, not occasional intensity.

- Stay Grounded: Let humility be your fuel. Remember what got you here—work ethic, sacrifice, and focus.

- Routine Rush: Build systems, not just ambition. Wake up with purpose even when there's no spotlight.

- Track Progress: Don't wait for others to notice— reflect on your journey. Celebrate when you improve 1%, not just when you win big.

"Success isn't what you do once. It's what you keep doing when no one's watching."

Breaking New Ground: Redefining What's Possible

Growth becomes stale without challenge. After reaching one goal, the mission becomes clear: break new ground.

- Set Higher Standards: Use past success as a new baseline, not a limit. Ask, "What's my next level of excellence?"

- Seek Discomfort: Real growth lives outside comfort zones. Push into areas you've avoided—public speaking, leading, innovating.

- Take Others With You: Progress accelerates when you bring people with you. Mentor someone. Start something. Build a legacy.

"If your goals don't scare you a little, they're not stretching you enough."

Tools for Long-Term Expansion

- Reflection Time: Weekly reflection helps keep the vision aligned. Ask: What worked? What didn't? What's next?

- Accountability Circle: Stay connected to people who challenge and support you.

- Fail Forward: Don't fear setbacks— they're part of progress. Each failure is data, not defeat.

Evolving Is a Lifestyle, Not a Phase.

When growth becomes part of who you are—not just what you do—you become unstoppable. You stop chasing milestones and start living in a mindset of expansion.

You begin to: See change as an opportunity. See struggle as training. See success as responsibility.

Final Words for the Journey Ahead

"Don't just maintain the fire. Build a bigger one. Keep climbing. Keep creating. Keep becoming."

This chapter marks the shift from achievement to impact—from rising for yourself to reaching back and lifting others. True advancement isn't just about personal wins; it's about how you use them. When positive change is sustained, it becomes a shared transformation. That's when a personal mission evolves into a movement.

You're no longer just building a better life for yourself—you're creating a ripple effect that can inspire and empower those around you.

Let that be your legacy.

Chapter 12: BUILDING BREAKTHROUGH DAILY HABITS - CHECKLIST FOR READERS:

– This is an example – customize it to fit your life.

Use this checklist to track your progress as you apply the key principles from "Your Success Routine: Breakthrough Success with Daily Habits."

Mindset & Language:

- ✓ Consider whether the words you use carry negative connotations.

- ✓ Shift from reactive to proactive language in daily situations (use the table as a reference from the book).

- ✓ Reflect on your responses each day—are you taking ownership or blaming external factors?

- ✓ Practice persistence, especially during setbacks.

Learning & Growth:

- ✓ Identify one new learning opportunity each week (e.g., podcasts, books, online courses).

- ✓ Emulate habits from role models mentioned (Examples - Chris Gardner, Justice Sotomayor) and others you admire.

- ✓ Set aside dedicated time every day for growth (even 10 minutes counts).

Generosity & Connection:

- ✓ Give generously each day—time, attention, or encouragement.

- ✓ Build a supportive circle and connect with others who share your goal of personal growth.

Routine Building:

- ✓ List 3-5 specific daily habits you want to build.

- ✓ Track these habits each day for at least four weeks.

- ✓ Regularly review and adjust routines based on what works and what doesn't.

Evidence & Reflection:

- ✓ Journal your wins and learnings once a week.

- ✓ Seek out credible resources or studies to reinforce your progress (psychology, habit formation research).

- ✓ Reflect on your personal stories of change; notice breakthroughs.

Actionable Steps:

- ✓ Create a checklist or framework for your own daily routines.
- ✓ Use "habit stacking"—link a new habit to something you already do.
- ✓ Celebrate small milestones along your journey.

Final Word

Breakthrough success is rarely about giant leaps — it's about showing up every single day. Your habits are the invisible architecture of your future. Build them with intention, nurture them with consistency, and watch your life transform one day at a time. No matter the obstacle, you've got this.

Appendix A.

You can always add more sheets later (like for utilities or subscriptions), but start with these four steps:

Step 1: The Planning Sheet

The first thing to do is list your annual income.

If you're salaried or hourly, write down your annual net salary. You will find your net pay per paycheck (the amount you actually receive after taxes and deductions). This is typically labeled as "Net Pay" or "Take-Home Pay" on your pay stub.

Don't include bonuses or one-time payments. It's better to be conservative and stick with the income you can count on.

Step 2: List All Your Expenses

Track Your Expenses (The Reality Check). Look at 2–3 months of bank and credit card statements. Categorize expenses into fixed (rent, utilities, insurance) and variable (groceries, dining, entertainment). Don't forget daily, weekly, monthly, quarterly, semi-annual, and annual. Use categories like:

- Car (loan, gas, insurance, repairs)

- Housing (rent/mortgage, maintenance, taxes)

- Utilities (electric, water, internet)

- Health (insurance, prescriptions)

- Food, clothing, entertainment, and more

Tip: Use an AI chatbot, a budgeting app, or use a current bank statement to help you brainstorm expenses you might forget.

Creating a budget doesn't have to be perfect at first. The important thing is to start—over time, you'll get better and better.

Step 3: Emergency Fund

Include a line item for an Emergency Fund. If possible, put aside 5% of each paycheck. If that's too much right now, start with whatever you can—even just a few dollars each pay period.

This is a mandatory part of your budget. Life is unpredictable. An emergency fund gives you a safety net.

Step 4: Long-Term Savings

Set up automatic transfers to savings for big future needs like a car or home. Try saving at least 5% of each paycheck or start with whatever you can. Even just a few dollars each pay period.

Automate it so it happens before you even see the money. Keeping this in a separate account makes it less tempting to use. Even small amounts add up faster than you think. Over time, you'll build a savings cushion without even feeling it.

Here's a clear explanation of weekly, biweekly, semimonthly, and annual in terms of pay or budgeting:

- Weekly (52 pay periods/year), you receive payment once a week.

- Biweekly (26 pay periods/year) You get paid every two weeks.

- Semimonthly (24 pay periods/year) You get paid twice a month — typically on fixed dates (e.g., the 15th and last day of the month). (See example below)

- Monthly (12 Pay periods/year.) (less common in the U.S. Total paychecks per year: 12.

Even though many people have similar expenses, everyone's budget is different. This planning sheet is just an example—you should choose what to include in your own budget. Check your bank statement to help guide you.

Now that you understand the basics, here's what a semimonthly (24 pay periods/year) Planning Sheet might look like:

Salary & Info	
Number of Paychecks Per Year	24
Annual Gross Salary	$50,000.00
Annual Net Salary (After Taxes)	$37,800.00
Net Paycheck Amount	$1,575.00
Sent to Savings Per Paycheck	$50.00
Net Paycheck Planning Amount	$1,525.00

← These values should match ↓

		Budget Total:	$1,525.00
Bill	Annual Cost	Monthly Cost	Cost Per Paycheck
Emergency Fund	$1,200.00	$100.00	$50.00
Car Loan	$3,600.00	$300.00	$150.00
Car - Gas	$1,560.00	$130.00	$65.00
Car - Insurance	$720.00	$60.00	$30.00
Car - Taxes	$480.00	$40.00	$20.00
House - Rent	$13,200.00	$1,100.00	$550.00
House - Rent Insurance	$480.00	$40.00	$20.00
Food	$7,200.00	$600.00	$300.00
Clothing	$480.00	$40.00	$20.00
Utilities (Internet, Heat, Electric, Cable)	$3,600.00	$300.00	$150.00
Cell Phone	$1,200.00	$100.00	$50.00
Health Co-pays	$480.00	$40.00	$20.00
Entertainment	$960.00	$80.00	$40.00
Student Loan	$1,200.00	$100.00	$50.00
Donations	$240.00	$20.00	$10.00
Visa	$0.00	$0.00	$0.00
Discover	$0.00	$0.00	$0.00

Now let's move on to building your "Budget" sheet. This sheet acts as your real-time view of your checking account and is the one you'll use most often. It tracks money coming in and going out, helping you stay on top of your finances day by day.

The amount of time you'll spend maintaining this sheet depends on how frequently you spend or deposit money—and how much control you want over your budget. As a general rule, it's a good idea to update your budget every two to three days to keep it current and accurate. This helps you:

- See what you've already spent

- Know how much money you have left

- Catch any unexpected charges quickly

Each time you receive a paycheck, you'll update your Budget sheet by adding the income amounts listed in your Planning sheet to the corresponding categories in your Budget sheet. If you're familiar with Excel macros, you can even automate this process, so it only takes one click.

Here's an example showing how your Budget sheet looks before and after adding a net paycheck of $1,525.00 to your checking account:

Previous Balance		→	After Paycheck	
Savings Account Balance	$50.00		Savings Account Balance	$100.00
Checking Account Balance	$1,195.00		Checking Account Balance	$2,720.00

Balance Total:	$1,195.00	Balance Total:	$2,720.00
Bill	Balance	Bill	Balance
Emergency Fund	$50.00	Emergency Fund	$100.00
Car Loan	$150.00	Car Loan	$300.00
Car - Gas	$10.00	Car - Gas	$75.00
Car - Insurance	$30.00	Car - Insurance	$60.00
Car - Taxes	$20.00	Car - Taxes	$40.00
House - Rent	$550.00	House - Rent	$1,100.00
House - Rent Insurance	$20.00	House - Rent Insurance	$40.00
Food	$20.00	Food	$320.00
Clothing	$10.00	Clothing	$30.00
Utilities (Internet, Heat, Electric, Cable)	$150.00	Utilities (Internet, Heat, Electric, Cable)	$300.00
Cell Phone	$50.00	Cell Phone	$100.00
Health Co-pays	$30.00	Health Co-pays	$50.00
Entertainment	$0.00	Entertainment	$40.00
Student Loan	$100.00	Student Loan	$150.00
Donations	$5.00	Donations	$15.00
Visa	$0.00	Visa	$0.00
Discover	$0.00	Discover	$0.00

Between paychecks, you may have pending transactions—like checks you've written or debit card purchases (such as for gas)—that haven't been processed yet. These delayed transactions can be confusing because your checking account might show more money than you actually have available.

To avoid this, it's essential to track and account for pending payments. For example, let's say you wrote a check for $1,100 to pay rent, but it hasn't been cashed yet. To stay accurate:

1. Subtract the $1,100 from your Rent category in your budget.

2. Record that same amount under a section called "Expected Payments."

This tells you the money is no longer available, even though it hasn't left your account yet. Once the check clears, you can remove it from the expected payments list and update your checking account balance accordingly.

Savings Account Balance	$100.00
Checking Account Balance	$2,720.00
Expected Payments Total:	-$1,100.00
Minus Expected Payments	$1,620.00

Numbers should equal

Balance Total:	$1,620.00
Bill	Balance
Emergency Fund	$100.00
Car Loan	$300.00
Car - Gas	$75.00
Car - Insurance	$60.00
Car - Taxes	$40.00
House - Rent	$0.00
House - Rent Insurance	$40.00
Food	$320.00
Clothing	$30.00
Utilities (Internet, Heat, Electric, Cable)	$300.00
Cell Phone	$100.00
Health Co-pays	$50.00
Entertainment	$40.00
Student Loan	$150.00
Tithing	$15.00
Visa	$0.00
Discover	$0.00

Expected Payments	
Check / Transaction	Balance
Check 1001 - Rent	$1,100.00

The last sheet we'll cover is the "Credit Card" section. In this sheet, simply list the name of each credit card you use and the specific bills that are paid with it. This helps you stay organized so that when your credit card bill is due, you know exactly which categories in your budget to pull money from to pay it off.

Credit Cards	
Credit Card	**Bill**
Visa	Utilities (Internet, Heat, Electric, Cable)
Visa	Cell Phone

For example, let's say you use your credit card to pay your monthly cell phone bill ($100) and utilities ($300). When your credit card bill arrives for $400, you would take $100 from the cell phone category in your budget and $300 from the utilities category, then use that money to pay the credit card bill in full.

The credit card sheet is especially helpful because it lets you track which expenses are charged to which cards. This makes it easier to notice changes in charges and quickly update your payment information if you ever get a new card or your card number changes.

Balance Total:	$2,720.00
Bill	Balance
Emergency Fund	$100.00
Car Loan	$300.00
Car - Gas	$75.00
Car - Insurance	$60.00
Car - Taxes	$40.00
House - Rent	$1,100.00
House - Rent Insurance	$40.00
Food	$320.00
Clothing	$30.00
Utilities (Internet, Heat, Electric, Cable)	$300.00
Cell Phone	$100.00
Health	$50.00
Entertainment	$40.00
Student Loan	$150.00
Donations	$15.00
Visa	$0.00
Discover	$0.00

Balance Total:	$2,720.00
Bill	Balance
Emergency Fund	$100.00
Car Loan	$300.00
Car - Gas	$75.00
Car - Insurance	$60.00
Car - Taxes	$40.00
House - Rent	$1,100.00
House - Rent Insurance	$40.00
Food	$320.00
Clothing	$30.00
Utilities (Internet, Heat, Electric, Cable)	$0.00
Cell Phone	$0.00
Health	$50.00
Entertainment	$40.00
Student Loan	$150.00
Donations	$15.00
Visa	$400.00
Misc	$0.00

You can create as many sheets as you need to help organize and track your expenses. In addition to tracking your credit cards, consider making a subscription sheet. This sheet will show how much you're spending on services like streaming platforms, gym memberships, or software subscriptions. You can also note the renewal dates so you can review or cancel them before you're charged again.

If you live in a place with cold winters or hot summers, your utility bills—like heat or electricity—are probably much higher during those extreme months. Instead of being surprised by a large bill, it's better to plan.

One helpful way to do this is to create a utilities sheet where you track your monthly costs from the previous year. Add up the total annual cost, then divide it by the number of paychecks you receive in a year. This tells you how much you need to set aside from each paycheck, so you're always prepared, even when the bills go up.

Here's an example of how to figure out how much to save for your electric bill based on last year's spending.

Electric Bill

Month	Cost
January	$50.00
February	$50.00
March	$50.00
April	$75.00
May	$75.00
June	$100.00
July	$250.00
August	$300.00
September	$100.00
October	$50.00
November	$50.00
December	$50.00
Annual Cost	**$1,200.00**

Annual Electric Cost / # of Paychecks
$1,200.00 / 24

Paycheck Amount: $50.00

Once your budget is set up, it won't take much time to keep it updated— carve out 15 minutes each week to focus on your budget — a small time investment that keeps your finances on track.". The more you use your budget, the better you'll get at predicting your expenses and managing your money. And as your budgeting skills grow, so will your sense of control. With that control comes something even more valuable: peace of mind and reduced financial stress.

Remember, there are many ways to create a budget sheet, and most banking apps offer tools to help you get started. One smart choice at a time—you got this with your finances.

Why Let the Bank Hold Your Money for Free? A Simple Lesson on Saving and Investing

There was a time, back in the 1980s and 1990s, when learning about saving and investing wasn't easy. There were no smartphones, no YouTube tutorials, no AI tools to break things down in plain language. If you wanted to understand how money worked, you had to ask around, go to the library, or rely on whatever the bank told you.

Back then, most people put their money into a regular savings or checking account. It felt safe — and it was. But what most didn't realize was this: the bank was using their money and barely paying them for it.

Even today, many people still don't question this. They let the bank hold their money without thinking about what *they're* getting in return. If your savings account is earning 1% interest or less, you're not making much, especially when inflation eats away at your money's value.

And here's another myth that still sticks around: "You need $10,000 or more to start investing."

Not true. You can start investing with just $500. One simple way is to put it in a CD — a Certificate of Deposit. It's low-risk and earns more interest than a regular savings account. Let's break it down:

- Principal (your deposit): $500

- Term: 12 months

- APY (Annual Percentage Yield): 5% (not 0.05 — that would be 0.05%, much lower)

- Interest earned after 1 year: $25.00

Instead of letting your $500 sit in an account earning $5 all year, you could earn $25 with no extra effort, just by being smarter about where you put your money. "That's growth—more than you had yesterday."

So, ask yourself: *Why let the bank hold your money without paying you fairly for it?* Before investing, make sure:

- You have no high-interest debt (like credit cards).

- You've saved up an emergency fund (3–6 months of expenses).

- You're not investing money you'll need in the short term (1–3 years).

If your job offers a 401(k) or 403(b) retirement plan, *enroll as soon as you can*—especially if your employer offers a match. That's *free money* added to your retirement savings just for participating. Even if you can only contribute a small amount, it adds up over time, and the earlier you start, the more you'll benefit from compound growth. You work hard for your money. It should work just as hard for you.

Acknowledgments

First and foremost, I give all honor and glory to God for the vision, the strength, and the grace to bring this book to life. This journey would not have been possible without divine guidance and favor every step of the way.

To my daughter, Theresa, and son DeVaughn, my husband Edward, and the children placed in my care who became part of my family —you are my greatest motivation. Your love, patience, and belief in me gave me the courage to keep going, even when it got tough. You reminded me of my "why."

To my family and friends, thank you for your unwavering support, for cheering me on, and for pushing me beyond my limits. Your encouragement and honest feedback helped shape this book into something real and meaningful.

Each of you played a vital role in this process, and for that, I am forever grateful.

About the Author

Charlene Swinton-Witkovic is the author of *Still Rising From Ashes*. Born in Harlem, New York, and later moving to the Bronx, she overcame a childhood marked by poverty to pursue higher education, earning her MBA from Central Connecticut State University. Charlene is a proud wife to Edward Witkovic and mother of two. She is passionate about empowering individuals to unlock their fullest potential by cultivating wealth, achieving vibrant health, and embracing financial freedom.

References

Benedict, J., & Jackson, C. (2023). *LeBron* [Audiobook]. Simon & Schuster Audio.

Blakely, S. (2022, August 30). *Sara Blakely bio: How the self-made billionaire invented Spanx*. MasterClass. https://www.masterclass.com/articles/sara-blakely-founder-of-spanx

Board of Governors of the Federal Reserve System. (2025). *Economic well-being of U.S. households in 2024: Banking and credit* (p. 56, Figure 28). https://www.federalreserve.gov/publications/files/2024-report-economic-well-being-us-households-202505.pdf

Brennan-Jobs, L. (2018). *Small fry: A memoir*. Alfred A. Knopf.

Dunwoody, A. E. (2015). *A higher standard: Leadership strategies from America's first female four-star general*. Hachette Books.

Dweck, C. S. (2006). *Mindset: The new psychology of success*. Random House.

Grant, A. (2013). *Give and take: A revolutionary approach to success.* Viking.

Hamilton, B., Berk, S., & Bundschuh, R. (2004). *Soul surfer: A true story of faith, family, and fighting to get back on the board.* MTV Books.

Haidt, J. (2024). *The anxious generation: How the great rewiring of childhood is causing an epidemic of mental illness.* Penguin Press.

Hill, N. (1937). *Think and grow rich.* The Ralston Society.

Isaacson, W. (2011). *Steve Jobs.* Simon & Schuster.

Jones, P. (2012). *The life of J.K. Rowling.* HarperCollins.

Kirkpatrick, D. (2010). *The Facebook effect: The inside story of the company that is connecting the world.* Simon & Schuster.

Levy, S. (2020). *Facebook: The inside story.* Blue Rider Press.

Mandela, N. (1994). *Long walk to freedom: The autobiography of Nelson Mandela*. Little, Brown and Company.

Mischel, W. (2014). *The marshmallow test: Understanding self-control and how to master it*. Little, Brown and Company.

Muccino, G. (Director). (2006). *The pursuit of happyness* [Film]. Columbia Pictures.

Perry, T. (2017). *Higher is waiting*. Random House Publishing Group.

Phelps, M., & Abrahamson, A. (2008). *No limits: The will to succeed*. Free Press.

Schultz, H., & Gordon, J. (2011). *Onward: How Starbucks fought for its life without losing its soul*. Rodale.

Sotomayor, S. (2013). *My beloved world*. Vintage Books.

Teladoc Health. (2024, April 1). *Whole foods vs. processed foods*. Harvard Health Publishing. https://www.bing.com/search?q=Teladoc+Health.+2

024.+"Whole+Foods+vs.+Processed+Foods."+Harvard+Health+Publishing

Vanity Fair. (2018, August 14). Lisa Brennan-Jobs' *Small Fry* tells the story of Steve Jobs' complicated fatherhood. https://www.vanityfair.com/news/2018/08/lisa-brennan-jobs-small-fry-steve-jobs-daughter

Washington, D. (2006). *A hand to guide me.* Meredith Books.

Winfrey, O. (2014). *What I know for sure.* Flatiron Books.

Yousafzai, M. (2013). *I am Malala: The girl who stood up for education and was shot by the Taliban.* Little, Brown and Company.

www.ingramcontent.com/pod-product-compliance
Lightning Source LLC
LaVergne TN
LVHW051602070426
835507LV00021B/2723